# The Rabbi, the Goddess, and Jung

# The Rabbi, the Goddess, and Jung

## GETTING THE WORD FROM WITHIN

Naomi Ruth Lowinsky

**The Rabbi, the Goddess, and Jung**
**Getting the Word from Within**

Copyright © 2016 by Naomi Ruth Lowinsky

First Edition

ISBN 978-1-77169-036-2 Paperback

ISBN 978-1-77169-037-9 eBook

All rights reserved. No part of this publication may be used or reproduced by any means, graphic, electronic, or mechanical, including photocopying, recording, taping or by any information storage retrieval system without the written permission of the publisher except in the case of brief quotations embodied in critical articles and reviews.

Published in the United States of America by Fisher King Press, an imprint of Fisher King Enterprises. For information on obtaining permission for use of material from this work, submit a written request to:

permissions@fisherkingpress.com

Fisher King Press
www.fisherkingpress.com
+1-307-222-9575

Many thanks to all who have directly or indirectly provided permission to quote their works. Every effort has been made to trace all copyright holders; however, if any have been overlooked, the author will be pleased to make the necessary arrangements at the first opportunity.

# CONTENTS

Acknowledgements — xi
Introduction — 1

## Section One: Her Tree Self
1. My Lady Tree — 5
2. Of Magical Maidens and Flowering Trees — 26

## Section Two: In the Dark of the Enigma
3. Getting the Word from Within — 47
4. The Devil and the Deep Blue Sea — 78

## Section Three: What is Africa to Me?
5. My Home is Over Jordan — 103
6. History is a Ghost Story — 125

## Section Four: Old Magic
7. The Rabbi, the Goddess, and Jung — 155
8. Drunk with Fire — 176

## Section Five: Grandmother Spider's Song
9. Earth Angel and the Tohu Bohu — 193

Bibliography — 215
Index — 221

*with deep gratitude to my Jungian lineage, especially Joe, Elizabeth, Gareth, and Betty*

*the spiritual seeker soon discovers he or she is not exploring something "up there," but rather the beyond that lies within.*[1]

---

[1] Daniel C. Matt, *The Essential Kabbalah*, p. 17.

# With Deep Gratitude

To the Elders
who blessed my beginnings, especially Joseph Henderson, Elizabeth Osterman, Mary Jo Spenser, June Singer, Donald Sandner, Lore Zeller, Gareth Hill, Betty Meador

To my Friends and Colleagues
fellow travellers on the spiral path, who inspire and support me, especially Sara Spaulding-Phillips, Sam Kimbles, Lou Vuksinick (whom I dearly miss), Jan Robinson-Vuksinick, Patricia Damery, Steven Nouriani, Ryan Bush, Richard Stein, Alicia Torres, Erel Shalit, Richard Messer, Leah Shelleda, Bill Fulton, Lynn Franco, Nate Kaufman, Carol Drucker, Andy Robbins, Cathy Valdez, Carolyn Cowan, Lucy Day

To the Editors of *Psychological Perspectives* and *The Jung Journal*,
who have encouraged my writing and given it a home, especially Gilda Frantz, Margi Johnson, Robin Robertson, Margaret Ryan, John Beebe, Steven Joseph, Dyane Sherwood, Katherine Olivetti

To Jane Zich
whose paintings of inner space have spoken to me for years, who graciously gave permission to use her magical painting, *Visionary 3*, on the cover of this book

To my Publishers, Mel Mathews and Patty Cabanas
who do so much to cultivate the creative imagination in Jungian writing, and who have given me a home for both prose and poetry for most of a decade. I am blessed by their friendship and know-how

To my children, step-children and grand children,
who bring me so much joy

and to my husband, Dan,
my ground and my sanctuary, curator of magical journeys, love of my life.

# INTRODUCTION

*Dreams pave the way for life, and they determine you without your understanding their language*[1]

A long time ago, when I was a candidate at the San Francisco Jung Institute, I dreamt a large lion prowled the Jung Institute Library. He told me he loved me. He told me he would eat me. That's a good summary of my story. For I have, indeed, been devoured by the fierce, wild energy of the living psyche as Jung understood it. Leo is my sun sign and my rising sign, astrologically. That lion is part of my nature.

It sounds painful to be eaten by a lion, to be torn apart by great teeth, to do time inside the dark gut of a predator. But what better description for how it feels when life forces you to surrender your conscious intent, throws you into the chaos of not knowing who you are or where you are going? Jungians—borrowing from alchemy—call this "the nigredo,"—the dark night of the soul. It happens in most people's lives and in most long Jungian analyses. It has happened, many times over, in mine.

I have learned, as in the famous story Martin Buber tells about himself, that I didn't have to account to God or my analyst for why I wasn't Moses, or for that matter, Jung. I had to account for why I wasn't Naomi. On the way to becoming myself, I came to see that though the library was my true habitat, I wasn't a big idea person, a great thinker and theorist. It was my calling as a writer and as an analyst to bring ideas into the living flesh of personal experience in a poetic way.

It's not enough to figure out your calling, your true nature. You have to know what time it is in your life. I was certified as a Jungian Analyst

---

1  C.G. Jung, *The Red Book*, p. 233.

in my 50th year. An intense period of study and psychological work—of being digested by the lion of my own nature—had come to fruition. It was time to reclaim my writing life, which had been put aside while raising my family, developing a practice, and becoming a Jungian Analyst. So proclaimed my Muse, The Sister from Below.

Now, in my 70s, I am informed by the chorus of inner figures who bring me word from within, that it's another kind of time in my life. Time to lie down with the lion and reflect on the journey; time to express my gratitude for the gifts of the Jungian Way—access to dreams and inner figures, access to the source of the word from within—my own wild and fierce creative spirit. It is harvest time—time to gather the fruits of my work and offer them as soul food to my community.

To that end, I have organized nine of my uncollected essays in this volume. As I've worked with these pieces—written over a period of fifteen years—I've been amused to see how the living symbols in my psyche have engaged and possessed me over the years. The Rabbi shows up early and shifts forms dramatically. So does the Goddess, the Lady Tree, and Jung. Words are magic, and getting the word from within is a spiritual practice, as are wild leaps into poetry.

Most of these essays were first published in *Psychological Perspectives* and the *Jung Journal*. One is a chapter in a book I co-edited with Patricia Damery, *Marked by Fire: Stories of the Jungian Way*. These are stories of *my* Jungian way, as an analysand, as an "apprentice to the alchemist"—Jung's term for the process of terminating an analysis—as a dreamer, a tree and goddess worshipper, a conflicted Jew, a conflicted Jungian, a mystic and a poet. Many of these essays loop back from different angles to the big dreams and origin stories that shaped me. I offer them to you, dear reader, in the hope they will support your own practice of getting the word from within.

# SECTION ONE

# HER TREE SELF

## Chapter 1

## My Lady Tree

*The creative urge lives and grows...like a tree in the earth...*[1]

### The Word Made Flesh

*Poetry is the art of letting the primordial word resound through the common word.*[2]

Words are magic. Look at the joy on a baby's face as she uses a word for the first time, and summons the ball she wants, the cookie, the mommy. Words give us power to influence others, to shape our lives. Words bring the stuff of our inner worlds—our feelings, thoughts, images, desires—out into the world of others. Words bring the raw stuff of emotion and experience into a focused form that we can share; they bring the prima material of the unconscious into consciousness; they tell our stories.

Words take us back to our cultural roots. "Every word was once a poem. Each began as a picture." So writes Wilfred Funk, author of

---

1 C.G. Jung, "On the Relation of Analytical Psychology to Poetry," *CW* 15, ¶ 115. Note: *CW* refers throughout this publication to *The Collected Works of C.G. Jung*.
2 Gerhart Hauptmann, quoted in Jung, "The Battle for Deliverance from the Mother," *CW* 5, ¶ 461.

the book, *Word Origins*. "Writing..." he tells us, "grows out of stylized drawing."[3] Robert Graves calls poetic practice "stored magic," turning words "into a living entity."[4]

The word "write," comes from a word that meant to scratch, which is what ancient people did with stone tools on birch bark.[5] Words then, take us back to old ways of seeing and knowing, to those ghostly spiritual worlds that haunt our language. The primordial word longs to surface, to bring the living symbol back to consciousness. For words contain images at their core, and as Jung informs us, "The symbolic process is an experience in *images and of images*."[6] Those images are stamped in our words.

In psychotherapy and Jungian analysis, our medium is language—the spoken word. Like poets we seek the "primordial word." We listen for the child in the adult, for the magic in her words that has been repressed, denied, cut off—for affect that longs to emerge. Jung writes:

> It is as if the poet could still sense, beneath the words of contemporary speech and in the images that crowd in upon his imagination, the ghostly presence of bygone spiritual worlds, and possessed the capacity to make them come alive again.[7]

The poet and the analyst have similar callings. We are both engaged in "getting the word from within." We listen for "bygone spiritual worlds" which haunt our words. We are engaged in the Promethean art of bringing life, fire, libido back to those words—so the symbol comes to life; the word is made flesh.

In the gospel according to St. John, it is said, "In the beginning was the Word, and the Word was with God, and the Word was God...And the Word was made flesh, and dwelt among us."[8] In the Jewish tradition, the world is created by the Word of God. The word is the breath of God, the eternal entering human flesh. It is said, "The Holy Spirit consists of

---

3  Wilfred Funk, *Word Origins*, pp. 1, 7.
4  Robert Graves, *The White Goddess*, p. 490.
5  Funk, *Word Origins*, p. 6.
6  Jung, "Archetypes of the Collective Unconscious," *CW* 9-1, ¶ 82.
7  Jung, "The Battle for Deliverance from the Mother," *CW* 5, ¶ 461.
8  *King James Bible*, Verses 1:1, 1:14.

three parts, Spirit, Voice and Word. From Spirit, God produced air and formed twenty-two sounds—the letters of the alphabet."[9]

In Hinduism the Word is a Goddess, Vac. Alain Daniélou quotes the Rig Veda:

> She…"enters into the seers." She gives power and intelligence to those she loves. She is the "mother of the Vedas," the consort of the lord-of-heaven…containing all the worlds within herself. "Hence Vac is everything…"
>
> Speech…[is] the daughter of Ritual-Skill…She is the wife of Vision…and the mother of the emotions…She also gives birth to the uncreated potentialities…She is…called the Hymn-to-the-Sun…called Gayatri at dawn, Savitri at midday, and Sarasvati at sunset.[10]

Robert Graves writes that in the ancient language of the Celts, the word "tree" means letter.[11] A poet was an "oak-seer."[12] Trees were poems and both were sacred to the Goddess. The word then, is sacred. In fact, the Word is divine, a God, or a Goddess!

## Becoming an Oak-Seer

> *This is the vowel of earth*
> *dreaming its root…*[13]
> —Seamus Heaney

I am haunted by a memory. When I was five or six I once drew a female figure—her arms reached upward; her feet were the roots of a tree; she was numinous to me. I called her my "Lady Tree." Proudly, I showed her to my father. He was a college professor, a musicologist. He could make music shine. He could make a Renaissance painting radiant with his

---

9 Howard Schwartz, *Tree of Souls*, p. 18.
10 Alain Daniélou, *The Myths and Gods of India*, pp. 260-261.
11 Graves, *The White Goddess*, p. 38.
12 Graves, *White Goddess*, p. 58.
13 Seamus Heaney, *Opened Ground*, pp. 117-118.

words, even to the eyes of a young child. But he couldn't see the beauty of my "Lady Tree."

"That's silly," he said. "Is it a bull?" The hurt of that moment is still palpable. I imagine we can all remember moments like that, when our young spirits were crushed.

Looking back I can see that my "Lady Tree" was a living symbol for me, an archetype that would shape my life and my fate. I had no idea then that the "Lady Tree" was both the goddess and her priestess, that she was sacred to the old religion in which the feminine is worshipped, that she was a divinity who would seek her way into flesh through me and many others of my time. I had no idea there was an ancient "Celtic Tree Alphabet" which Robert Graves argued was a secret code by which poets handed down their worship of the forbidden White Goddess. I had no idea that in Africa, a young man, Malidoma Somé—who was to become a well known shaman—would see the Goddess in the Tree, while undergoing his initiatory rites. He would recognize Her body glowing with green, as an expression of Her "immeasurable love."[14] I had no idea that the goddess was associated with trees in cultures all over the world, no idea that in the Middle Ages the tree was addressed with the honorific "Lady,"[15] or that Hildegard of Bingen had married two words—"green" and "truth" to coin the word "veriditas,"[16] to describe the moment God heals you with a plant. I had no idea that the Tree of Life was the sacred glyph of Jewish mysticism, or that I would spend much of my life reclaiming the living symbol of my "Lady Tree"—she would come to me in dreams, in life, in poems—she was the primordial form of my shape-shifting muse, "The Sister from Below."[17]

I had no idea that just a few years later I would find a tree to sit in—an oak—which would become my friend, my familiar, and in its branches I would begin to write poems. I had no idea I was becoming an oak-seer, haunted by the spiritual world of the Druids. I had not

---

14 Malidoma Somé, *Of Water and the Spirit*, p. 224.
15 Jung, "Symbols of the Mother and of Rebirth," *CW* 5, ¶ 368.
16 Hildegard of Bingen, *Meditations with Hildegard of Bingen*, p. 17.
17 Naomi Ruth Lowinsky, *The Sister from Below*.

read Deena Metzger's wonderful book about writing practice, *Writing for Your Life*, or her description of the World Tree:

> ...with its roots in the underworld and its branches in the heavens, it is a portrait of the relationship of the worlds to each other, and the process of passing from one to another. The beanstalk, the ladder, the *axis mundi*, the cross, the grove of the goddess, the tree of life, the tree of the knowledge of good and evil in the garden and the Kabbalistic Tree of Life are variations on this fundamental teaching.[18]

How could I have known then, that I was not only carrying the wound of a little girl whose father mocked her "Lady Tree," I was carrying the wound of generations of women held in a patriarchal worldview that cut them off from their primordial roots in the earth, their arms that reached for the sky. I had no idea that other little girls were visited by Trees. One of them was Deena Metzger, who wrote her first poem when she was three, about a tree. She writes:

> With words, the little girl at three brought an invisible tree into view...How did the little girl learn of the tree she wrote about? She hadn't been told of its existence. It wasn't in a picture book, a botanical magazine, or the dictionary. It wasn't part of the family folklore. She didn't learn about it at school... She must have found it in herself...
>
> As an older woman, when I finally remembered the tree, I remembered the knowledge of that tree, the vastness of the realm of the imagination. I know now that imagination is the domain of the inner world and that the creative is the way to it.[19]

Two women who have never met were visited in childhood by the same living symbol. For both it augured their later creative life. Both would forget the Tree for many years, and for both, remembering it, would reunite the older woman and the little girl.

---

18  Deena Metzger, *Writing for Your Life*, p. 151.
19  Metzger, *Writing for Your Life*, pp. 3-4.

Years later, I came upon the strange fact that my father was on to something when he wondered whether my "Lady Tree" was a bull. I learned, reading Marija Gimbutas, that the bull was sacred to the forgotten goddess. Its head and upwardly curved horns were symbolic of the reproductive organs of a woman: uterus and fallopian tubes.[20] But, the little girl in me insists, he didn't know the primordial image behind the word. He was teasing, and being mean.

As a mature woman, I kept being guided back to my "Lady Tree." I had a dream of a root vegetable, a potato or a parsnip, wearing a gauzy summer dress. A voice informed me that this was Helena. When I happened upon this living symbol in a museum in Macedonia—an ancient clay goddess, I recognized her as a form of my "Lady Tree."

I stumbled upon a "Lady Tree" in Orissa, India, on the side of the road—a huge banyan tree, where I was told, ladies could relieve themselves. The tree had been made sacred by the presence of a dark goddess, made of cloth, dressed in gorgeous silk, bedecked with jewels, and provided fresh offerings of fruit and flowers. It has taken me most of a lifetime and two long analyses to learn to trust the charged path of the living symbol, and how to follow it into the making of poems. How that happened is the story I want to tell.

## Donkey in the Basement

*Symbols act as transformers.*[21]

In the late 1960s a young woman entered a Jungian analysis. What brought her in? She had had a terrible dream. She dreamt that her three-year-old daughter's head was severed from her body. She heard her mother's voice say: "You'll never get her together again." This young woman was a fragmented soul, split off from the surge of her libido, cut off from the meaning of her words, severed from her authenticity and from her gods. She was incarcerated in taboos and constrictions that blocked her feeling, stole her breath, smothered her fire. She had for-

---

20  Marija Gimbutas, *The Language of the Goddess*, p. 265.
21  Jung, *CW* 5, ¶ 344.

gotten her "Lady Tree," forgotten her early call to write poems. She was recently returned from two years in India, a culture teeming with living symbols which took her over, played with her, seduced her, ate her alive. She was in thrall to the Hindu pantheon, had no idea how to integrate Krishna, Kali, Ganesha, Sarasvati, into an American life. They made nonsense of any notion she had had of becoming a college professor, like her father. She was lost, had no idea how to support herself, how to be a contributing member of the culture; she had no idea who she was.

She dreamt that the fortress in which she lived was blown down by a great wind, or toppled by an earthquake. She dreamt there was a nasty donkey in her childhood basement—kicking at the sterile tiled walls. Over the course of many years, through the circumambulations and meanderings of two analytic conversations, this woman found her way back to the passionate flow of her life, her own primordial word, her living symbol, her "Lady Tree." At the end of her second analysis, she had a dream of a blossoming tree; she was given a large yellow flower. She had found her way into the world, become a Jungian analyst. And she had found her way into her own inner world, reclaimed her goddess, answered the call of her muse.

That analysand, of course, was me.

Jung defines symbols as "shaped energies…whose effective power is just as great as their spiritual value."[22] He writes that, "a living symbol… [expresses] the inexpressible in unsurpassable form…" So does a poem.

The "Lady Tree" certainly feels like a "shaped energy." It had great power over me, still does. I had no idea what she meant when she first came to me. She is still revealing herself to me—a lifetime later. She made no sense to my father and so he chopped her down with the hatchet of his skeptical mind. For the realm of symbols and of images has been pushed into the unconscious by our cultural insistence on the rational. It is the work of a Jungian analysis to free the psyche to entertain its images, to track dreams, to follow the intense numen of the living symbol. As Jung says, "a practical advantage of no small consequence is gained, namely, the *collaboration of the unconscious*."[23] If, with Jung, we

---

22 Jung, "The Type Problem in Poetry, *CW* 6 ¶ 425.
23 Jung, "Schiller's Ideas on the Type Problem," *CW* 6 ¶ 204.

understand the unconscious as the divine, you can see how significant this "practical advantage" is—it gets you collaborating with your gods.

A successful Jungian analysis is a subversive business, smashing taboos, opening prison gates, encouraging freedom of speech and association, wild leaps of thought and image, access to the imaginal realm. It provides a sanctuary for the development of an inner life, a safe place in which the child within the grown woman can discover her own story, reclaim what her childhood repressed. Her voice is honored, she learns to use her words, to say her passionate truths; her spirit is recognized; she is free to worship her personal goddess. For, as Deena Metzger writes, the inner world is, "vast, endless and complex. It is the world of worlds. It is infinite. To enter it is…to learn of the boundlessness of the self."[24]

When you've been listened to deeply, openly, you begin to listen to yourself. You allow yourself to hear the wild, nasty, weird thoughts and fantasies you have. You are no longer so afraid of your shadow. You learn to follow the intricate twists and turns of your own very peculiar mind, your strange dreams, your colorful fantasies. If it is in your nature, perhaps you begin to make something of them—music, art, poetry. Here is a poem I wrote about my first analysis. It came to me in the manner of a life review, toward the end of my second analysis.

### letter to a first analyst

*I caught the dream*
    *and rose dreaming*
        *—H.D.*

He sat with me in the early years   when it was all
coming apart   my too young marriage
that business of the donkey
in the basement   the father whose eyes entered
me   took what they would

He sat with me   and I opened like a window
in a suffocating room   whose drapes

---

24  Metzger, *Writing for Your Life*, p. 7.

have been drawn for too long
now blinds snapped up   smell of hot tomatoes
                              strawberries in the sun

                    I had been living
in my body   as though it were an unmade bed
for years   the smell of decomposing
dreams under the bedside table   crumpled kleenex
bad blood spotting
the sheets       the children were so little they wandered in
wanting their breakfast     and me just waking from a dream
of spitting out my teeth on the road or dream of using
a contact lens for contraception    It splintered
inside me   What spirit led me to him   after the terrible dream
my daughter's head was severed
from her body       my mother's voice said: "you'll never
                              get her together again"

I write to tell him that I danced at that daughter's wedding
on a hillside in Berkeley   not far from his house     She
was beautiful     and I was glad for all the years
of catching the morning dream   the hours he sat with me
through sandstone storms and backdoor men   Even death's
most yellow incarnation made a pass at my bed    but he
who opened windows   closed that door    I remember

once he told me the story of a prince   and a hairy wild man
fresh out of the forest    They wrestled for a long time
   fought        until each knew the other's  body and mind
until they were   inseparable
                    friends[25]

    That donkey in the basement was doing essential work, breaking down the walls of convention and expectation, opening the psyche to the dark earth, the mysteries, the ground waters of the unconscious. The donkey, in my personal association, was both a nasty name my father called my mother, (in German—"du Esel!") and my mother's stubborn, strong nature. She was the beast of burden in the family, who kept everything going and got little recognition for it. That sterile basement

---

25  Lowinsky, first published in *Rattle*.

had to be broken into by my shadow issues, the living roots, dirt, and chaos of the underworld.

I can imagine, having sat in the analyst's chair for many years now, how difficult it must have been for my analyst to sit "with me…when it was all coming apart." He had to sit with my chaos and confusion, my pain and terror, my furiously kicking donkey. It is essential, I have learned, not to interfere with the process of disorientation, to allow the fragmentation, the disintegration that will eventually open up the windows of that suffocating room and let in the smell of hot tomatoes and strawberries. I am grateful to him for letting it happen.

It is also difficult to know the moment to make an offering, a symbolic gift to orient the wandering soul. My analyst gave me the gift of a myth—the story of the powerful prince Gilgamesh and the hairy wild man from the forest, Enkidu—how they wrestled, until "they knew each other's body and mind, until they were inseparable friends." It was a vessel, a framework in which I could understand my own conflict between the wild one in me who shook her fist at the establishment, and the ambitious young woman who wanted to make her way in the world. That myth has held me for many years. It has enabled two very different inner figures of the masculine—who vie for my devotion—to work out their differences, as friends. The poet Robert Bly describes what that myth did for me:

> In the epic of Gilgamesh, which takes place in a settled society, psychic forces suddenly create Enkidu, "the hairy man," as a companion for Gilgamesh, who is becoming too successful. The reader has to leap back and forth between the white man, "Gilgamesh" and the "hairy man."[26]

It was the work of that first analysis to help me find my way into the world, and into a relationship with my inner "hairy man" and my inner prince. It was the work of my second analysis, begun as I was considering applying to the Jung Institute, to bring me back to my inner life, and to my calling as a poet.

---

26  Robert Bly, *Leaping Poetry*, p. 1.

## The Real Story

> *In the history of symbols this tree is described as the way of life itself, a growing into that which eternally is and does not change.*[27]

There was a time when I thought I needed to choose between being an analyst and being a poet. As I wrote of my muse in "The Sister from Below":

> I thought She was a distraction, a frivolity. Who has time for poetry when the world is such a perilous place? And anyway, She was making a shambles of my life. She'd blast me with intense images, or send me careening off, intoxicated with the power of some word; I'd not be heard from for hours; the dishes wouldn't get done. The children's dinner wouldn't get cooked. I had to send Her into exile.[28]

It was the gift of my second analysis to learn that, for me, being an analyst and being a poet are two sides of the same coin, two aspects of the same "Lady Tree." Poetry and analysis are both concerned with the integrity of language, its resonance into the depths, its capacity to hold strong feeling, leaping images—the primordial word. Robert Bly writes that the power of the "image is the power of seeing resemblances… Remembering forgotten relationships is then one of the great joys that comes from making up poetry."[29]

During that second analysis I was flooded with images of forgotten and taboo relationships—the goddess, my own body. Thankfully, I was in the company of a woman analyst who knew the realm of body and goddess well and could sit with me as I struggled for language. Here's a poem about that symbolic process:

---

27  Jung, "Psychological Aspects of the Mother Archetype," *CW* 9-1, ¶ 198.
28  Lowinsky, *The Sister from Below*, p. 5.
29  Bly, "What the Image Can Do," *Claims for Poetry*, p. 43.

### she of the attic fire

of witch's oven
of seven lost clay tablets
> has become my familiar

> Who can say how
> > this happened?

> That they unearthed her
> enigmatically smiling face
> > > at Troy?

> That she danced topless in a bar
> > named Babylon
> > > singing Innana's
> > > > vulva song?

> That she went bottomless
> into the pit     riding the devil's
> > hard knuckled cock

> That she was swallowed
> by the dragon     or was it a whale?

> That it took her two times seven
> years    to tunnel her way out
> to scrape lost syllables
> > > off the rocks
> to lure her tongue back
> from the cattails in the swamp

> to translate
> > what  belly knows
> > into words
> > that can be said
> > between two sitting women
> > > in a quiet room?[30]

---

30 Lowinsky, *crimes of the dreamer*, p. 31.

One cannot see ahead on the path of a long analysis. The way reveals itself as one walks it. Passion and grief need expression. The living symbol finds its way into one's words. Inner figures emerge to lead one into what one does not yet know—a magnetic pull into one's deep life, into a wisdom that is larger than one's conscious attitude, into a poem you didn't know was in you—bringing together dreams, memories and collective events, such as the archeological discoveries that unearthed Troy.

The analyst is a tracker in the internal wilderness, following you into "the pit," helping you turn the scary witch of childhood into a "familiar," helping you "lure your tongue back from the cattails in the swamp," supporting the expression of transgressive fantasies, listening to the deeper level, the "real story" in which you live an ancient, now forbidden life.

**in the real story**

>you are a dancing girl
>a devadesi   from the temple at Jaipur
>or maybe it is Ur
>the sacred fire's been lit
>I've taught you how
>to catch your own sweet pulse

>>you await the stranger
>>who crosses the desert
>>>on a red mare
>>two moons this night
>>your hands on his back
>>your soles on the stones
>>you drink
>>>the milky way

>>in the real story
>>your open thighs reveal
>>>the crescent

moon[31]

The real story takes place in an eternal realm where the sacred and the erotic have not been severed, where women are trained in the erotic arts— love, music and poetry, a realm in which there are dancing girls in the temples at Jaipur, or maybe it is Ur: maybe it is Lesbos, and Sappho is our love and poetry teacher. Bly tells us, "the Middle Ages were aware of a relationship between a woman's body and a tree."[32] My poem revealed to me the forgotten relations between sky and open thighs. In the eternal realm of the imagination, which my second analysis unlocked for me, the "Lady Tree" became the Philosophical Tree of my development, my access to inner realms in which a topless dancer knows Inanna's vulva song.

Every analysis takes a different path, through different internal and external landscapes; every analysand expresses him or herself in different words, with different symbols. For some, the dream will carry the living symbol; for others, it emerges in the analytic relationship. When one is listened to deeply, understood, and one's spirit is invited to come out of its hiding place in the family or cultural closet, the living image is free to leap into the word itself, to fill it with its primordial resonance.

One of the ways this happens is in the working through of empathic failures, those gut-wrenching moments for an analyst when you hear yourself sounding like your patient's most negative inner voice. Here is a poem about that:

### this strange practice

>one chair
>one couch
>one talks to oneself
>>in the presence of another
>
>>dreams come
>>visitations from

---

31 Lowinsky, *crimes of the dreamer*, p. 27.
32 Bly, "What the Image Can Do," *Claims for Poetry*, p. 42.

> the witch
> her gathumping shoes
> on the other side
> of childhood
>
> also the wolf
> his dinner table teeth
>
> how can a quiet room become
> a belly full
> of misery?
>
> and she
> her tongue
> gone wrong
> is now the one who
> (same old story)
> snicker snack your cut out heart
> is dropped
> into a bag
> of shame until
>
> next hour
> one who was seen but not heard
> pours out a belly full of ache
> one who can hear
> sends breath to belly
>
> hot blood
> to your heart[33]

Here the living symbol is in the word made flesh: the "belly full of ache," the "breath to belly, hot blood to your heart." The word may simply be "No!" The bad child, the rebel angel, the devil, the prodigal who has been cast out, cut off, exiled from love, from consciousness, from power in the world, who hangs out in the unconscious making trouble, intruding on dreams, beating up children, creating messes, comes out into the light, yells "No" at her analyst, is rude, badly behaved, stands

---

33 Lowinsky, first published in *Edgz*.

up for her own fierce truth, for the magic of her Lady Tree. This is how her spirit is freed, the God within renewed, her libido released.

For me, the word could not be made flesh, the holy could not enter my words, until I'd spent years letting the nasty, the shameful, the taboo out into the open air of my analytic sanctuary. Until my words could be their loud full-bodied irreverent selves I could not claim them for myself, could not take them seriously, could not let them lead me into the deep woods. Cleansed of shame, freed from constrictions, let out of the closet, my words could go where they would, imagine whatever they fancied, do the hootchy-koochy if they were so inclined—often they did.

One way of understanding the transformative processes of analysis is that, when it works it brings the Holy Spirit of an analysand into manifestation. She finds her voice, is able to express her words, her truth, has access to a set of living symbols—the "Lady Tree," the attic fire, the witch who rides the devil's cock, the topless bar named Babylon—that fill her world with meaning.

She and her analyst have created a private language, a personal Tarot deck of living symbols, born of their shared wanderings in her internal landscape—her Gods and demons, dreams, memories, wounds, and longings. This is the stuff of her soul. Together they come to know what moves her, what excites her, how her words become flesh. Perhaps she will find a creative form in which to express the power of her personal symbols.

## When Trees Become Women

> *Creativity is the most mysterious quality of the human, and it has the strongest affinity with the divine.*[34]

The opus of tracking the living symbol has continued for me years past two long analyses, into the work I do with myself—the daily spiritual practice of translating the spoken word, the image glimpsed in reverie or dream, into the written form of a poem, or these prose reflections.

---

34  Metzger, *Writing for Your Life*, p. 156.

I have had to learn to sit with my own chaos, to free myself to leap wildly, to track my strange inner images, to talk to inner figures. Though from time to time I have remembered the "Lady Tree," and been struck by how my father's mockery still smarts, I had not understood, until I began wrestling with this essay, her history in me, her continuing power over my life and fate, her work to make a forgotten spiritual world come to life.

She is not, as in so many Greek myths, a woman becoming a tree in order to escape some lusty Pan of the woods. She is tree becoming woman, reaching into the psyche of a young girl to connect the human and natural worlds. She harks back to Celtic wisdom—she is the manifestation of the Tree Alphabet, word becoming flesh.

Jung says: "We must…let things happen in the psyche…This is an art of which most people know nothing. Consciousness is forever interfering, helping correct, and negating."[35] This, in an acorn shell, is what I learned in analysis, and what I keep teaching myself again and again in my writing practice. It is the Secret of the Golden Flower, the wisdom of the Philosophical Tree, the sine qua non of the creative process. Jung describes it as a process of paying close attention to one's fantasies. He writes:

> The way of getting at the fantasies varies with individuals. For many people, it is easiest to write them down; others visualize them, and others again draw or paint them…
>
> These exercises must be continued until the cramp in the conscious mind is relaxed, in other words, until one can let things happen…In this way a new attitude is created, an attitude that accepts the irrational and the incomprehensible simply because it is happening.[36]

Jung teaches that our relationship with the living symbols in our lives can be cultivated by the practice of active imagination. In active imagination, you do not only watch what is happening in your psyche, you engage with it—you have a conversation with an inner figure. My book,

---
35 Jung, "Commentary on the *Secret of the Golden Flower*," *CW* 13, ¶ 20.
36 Jung, "Commentary on the *Secret of the Golden Flower*," *CW* 13, ¶¶ 20-23.

*The Sister from Below,* is a series of acts of imagination. It seems only fair that I should engage my "Lady Tree" in such a dialogue.

As Jung says, people have different ways of working with their fantasies. My way is writing. With pen and notebook, I invoke whatever figure I want to hear from and ask for a response. I never know what I'm going to write until I've written it—or more accurately—until I've read what's been written by a consciousness greater than my ego.

So, Lady Tree, tell me who you are, why you came to me young, why you hid yourself so long, what you want from me now?

The Lady Tree appears, as she did when I was a child. She is a green magnetism that is uncannily similar to the smiling green lady Malidoma Somé encounters in the course of his shamanic initiation.[37] She is the personification of Hildegard's *veriditas* and the greening of Robert Graves' White Goddess—a numinous lady who speaks to me:

*I am your primordial image, your essential self—too obvious, too holy for you to appreciate until you had been initiated into your deep life. I have always been with you, but you have forgotten me, ignored me, dismembered me. I am your upward and downward reaching, your world tree, your passion for what can't be seen and what is everywhere seen in the natural world. I am the shape of your fate, the tongue of your craft, your "stored magic," your secret talisman reminding you of who you were before you were born and who you will be when you pass out of your fleshly form. I visit your dreams. Remember when Emma Jung showed up and gave you a T shirt with a great oak painted upon it? She said it was your "Tree of Life" and that you should wear it for your meeting with the certifying committee—the committee which was to decide if you were ready to become a Jungian Analyst. You got certified. Remember the upside down tree, made of Hebrew letters—roots in the sky, branches touching the earth—that I revealed to you in a dream? I told you to study the Kabbalah. You learned to meditate upon the mystical tree and its ten sefirot—to understand the complex flow of energy between heaven and earth, to recognize the Goddess in Judaism. This, and your writing practice, held you after you ended analysis; it holds you still. That is me. I am your Philosophical Tree—your Golden Flower.*

---

37  Malidoma Somé, *Of Water and the Spirit*, p. 221.

*I am the sap that rises in you, that wants to find words for what cannot be said—your yearning for the beyond and the below—your word song, your trance, your incantations. I am your roots that reach below ground water, your arms that reach to touch sky. What I want from you now is a poem—a new poem that recognizes the time when trees were women and trees were poems—a poem that sings of our lifelong kinship, yours and mine, the songs I've sung you, how I animate your world. Give me your voice as though it were song. Give me your spirit as though you were green. Sing me a chorus. I want my word made flesh.*

So the Lady Tree has demanded a poem. This turned out to be easier said than done. Some poems just come. Others require wrestling with a difficult angel. It wasn't easy finding a way to bring her green spirit into manifestation, her holiness into form. This is true in analysis, and in the writing of poems.

Symbols, I find, yearn to be embodied. But bodies fear their power. Bodies are great clunky things, awkward in the presence of the unseen. When I'm working on a poem and it's not going well, I feel off-center, chaotic, irritated. My body knows something is off. For the body has its wisdom and the word made flesh is profoundly physiological.

When the poem comes to fruition, feels complete, when it has become itself, one feels the kind of relief, release, associated with certain bathroom and bedroom activities. The poet Edward Hirsch, explains it this way: "The spiritual life wants articulation—it wants embodiment in language. The physical life wants the spirit."[38]

A poem, like a living symbol, expresses the inexpressible. In Deena Metzger's words: "A poem is a penetration into the essence of something."[39] Or in the words I quoted in the beginning of this essay: "Poetry is the art of letting the primordial word resound through the common word." The poet seeks to make "bygone spiritual worlds"… "come alive again."

Here is the poem commissioned by my "Lady Tree."

## A Life in Trees

---

38  Edward Hirsch, *How to Read a Poem*, p. 6.
39  Metzger, *Writing for Your Life*, p. 156.

## I. Oak

Queen of the dark down under
and of bright in the sky
my little girl legs remember
your lap     Sun sang in your limbs
When I sat in your spell
words were your birds
twig feather leaf blossom

It gets lonely
so lonely
without you

## II. Willow

Lady of river
and swamp     I remember
your long green hair     what it kindled
in me—your tongue in my ear
my body your flute
how snake became
my sister

It feels hollow
so hollow
without you

## III. Palm

Your long legged dance
Enchanting the edge
of tomorrow     You give birth
to the Buddha
lift my eyes to the mountain
how it comes     how it goes
while the river flows

It's barren
so barren
without you

## IV. Dismembered

the ones who've been cut down
stunted     never blossomed
those ripped from their grounds
without solace
complain to the wind
And the wind throws
their buckets of sorrow
into this poem

Are there words
that can bear
such grievance?

## V. Lady Tree

You have written the book
of life     Your roots know sky
Your branches know down
below ground water
You drink from my dreams
Remember me oak willow palm
Remember me buckets of sorrow
Give me twig feather leaf bird
Give me word
        that bursts
                into flower[40]

---

40  Lowinsky, *The Faust Woman Poems*, pp. 39-41.

## Chapter 2

## Of Magical Maidens and Flowering Trees[1]

> *It is only after a fateful journey to a...strange land, that the meaning of the inner voice that is to guide our quest can be revealed to us.*[2]

### The Queen of the Night

> *A tree that has come to flower or fruit...is treated as a mother, a woman who has given birth.*[3]

"Children, I want to tell you a story," sings the storyteller at the beginning of John Adams' opera, *A Flowering Tree*. We are invited into worlds we knew as children, worlds of "once upon a time," of "make believe," of the creative imagination, where children play, where souls are healed, where anything can happen. Jung describes this world as "esse in anima," of being in the soul, and he tells us it is the "only primordial

---

[1] Lowinsky, published in an earlier form in the *Jung Journal*, Vol. 2, Number 1, 2008.
[2] Heinrich Zimmer, *Myths and Symbols in Indian Art and Civilization*, p. 221.
[3] A.K. Ramanujan, "A Flowering Tree: A Woman's Tale," *Collected Essays*, p. 423.

phenomenon accessible to us, the real Ground of the psyche."[4] In the poetic words of the libretto, we are ushered into a "time of honey and elephants," where a magical young woman can transform herself into a flowering tree and then back into her human form.[5]

In his eloquent meditations on Indian poetry and lore, the translator of this South Indian folktale, A.K. Ramanujan, reflects on mirrors that become windows, on stories that reflect on one another, on poems and folktales that reflect the great Hindu epics. In Indian poetry, he remarks that, "every poem resonates with the absent presence of others that sound with it, like the unstruck strings of a sitar. So we respond to a system of presences and absences…"[6] I think this is how we respond in general to art, to music, to stories. It's the meandering path of personal association we Jungians bring to dreams; it's the circumambulation of cultural and archetypal resonances we call amplification. This is the path I invite you to take with me. Children, I want to tell you stories about stories, stories within stories, some from my own life, in response to this enchantment of an opera, *A Flowering Tree*.

Once upon a time when I was a little girl, growing up in a family whose true religion was music, I remember sitting at the kitchen table of our brick row house in Queens, listening to Mozart's *The Magic Flute* on the radio—perhaps a live performance broadcast from the Met, for I recall that kind of excitement was in the air. Usually my father would hold forth about music. He was, after all, a professor of musicology. But this time I remember my mother, whose wisdom came from the heart, explaining to me that the Queen of the Night was trying to find her daughter. The queen's great coloratura aria, with its wild leaps into high ranges, its intensity, its mystery, has stayed with me ever since. I was enchanted. The Queen of the Night became a powerful character in my imaginal landscape. I did not know then that she represented the forces of darkness to the Enlightenment mind. Nor did I know that much later I would become a devotee of that dark goddess.

---

4   Jung, *Letters*, Vol. I, p. 60.
5   Libretto by John Adams and Peter Sellars. *A Flowering Tree*.
6   Ramanujan, "Where Mirrors are Windows," *Collected Essays*, p. 15.

My mother told me about the prince's magic flute. She told me that the ordinary fellow, Papageno, the one who stood for us everyday folk, had a Panpipe, which was a kind of magic too. I was too young to understand the meaning of the opera's setting in ancient Egypt, nor its arcane references to secret Masonic rituals involving fearful initiations. I did not know that someday I would become a Jungian analyst, well-versed in fearful initiations.

When I learned that *A Flowering Tree* was commissioned by Peter Sellars as part of the great multicultural festival of music, dance, and film to celebrate the 250th anniversary of Mozart's birth he organized, and that he had asked John Adams for an opera in the spirit of Mozart and *The Magic Flute,* the "unstruck strings" of my sitar began to resonate. On top of this, while I was deeply engaged in writing this paper, my mother, who knew nothing of what I was working on, called to wish me happy Mozart's birthday. She had never before mentioned that she is one of a musical group who gather every year to play Mozart for hours on his birthday!

But what, I wondered, is the deeper story about this American composer, whose works, *Nixon in China, The Death of Klinghoffer,* and *Dr. Atomic,* have responded to our public agonies, the terrors of the twentieth century, the Faustian bargain we've made for power over the earth and her secrets? What possessed him to go wandering off into an ancient South Indian folktale? The spirit of Mozart could have taken him in many directions. Why this one? If we believe, with Jung, that artists "are always the first to divine the darkly moving mysterious currents and… stirrings of the collective unconscious,"[7] what could Adams and Sellars be divining? Does the story carry in it seeds of what we need for our own troubled times? Is there a secret in it, as Goethe, Mozart's fellow Mason, indicated there was in *The Magic Flute* when he said: "It is enough that the crowd would find pleasure in seeing the spectacle; at the same time, its high significance will not escape the initiates."[8]

---

7  Jung, "The Type Problem in Poetry," *CW* 6, ¶ 321.
8  Grand Lodge of British Columbia and Yukon.

## Seeds from Long Ago

> *Six grains were whole*
> *ten thousand*
> *years after their time…*[9]

Here's another story: Once upon a time in faraway Mysore, South India, a son was born to a Tamil Brahmin family. His name was A.K. Ramanujan. He listened to the stories of the father world. His father quoted the Vedas in Sanskrit; he quoted Shakespeare in English. His father was a scientist and an astronomer. To his son's consternation, he also believed in astrology and seemed to have no problem mixing rational and irrational approaches to the stars. Ramanujan listened to the stories of the mother world told in Kannada and Tamil. He would later distinguish between what he called "father language" and "mother tongue."[10] *A Flowering Tree* would never have come into being, had not some mysterious spirit moved him to collect the folktales told by the women of his childhood, before he knew there was such a thing as the academic study of folklore. He took it upon himself to bring the rich lore of the mother tongue to the printed page and the college classroom.

There is a story of my own embedded in this one: Once upon a time, when I was just beginning to settle into my own calling as a poet, I read a poem of A.K. Ramanujan's in *Poetry* magazine. It resonated with many unstruck strings in my soul. Who was this poet with the Indian name who could evoke the power of what had been buried long ago so elegantly? He became another character in my imaginal landscape, a fellow poet of "esse in anima," of being in the soul. His poem "Foundlings in the Yukon" told the story of a miracle: some seeds, held in the skeleton of a lemming and sealed off by a landslide in Pleistocene times, had been discovered by miners in the Yukon and planted. In the words of the poem:

> they took root
> within forty-eight hours

---

9  Ramanujan, *Collected Poems*, p. 156.
10  Ramanujan, *Collected Essays*, p. xv.

and sprouted...

as if long deep
burial had made them hasty

for birth and season...like
this morning's dream of being
born in an eagle's
nest with speckled eggs and the screech
of nestlings, ...or maybe
just elegies in Duino unbound
from the dark...[11]

Ramanujan shape-shifted dramatically in my imagination when he showed up in my bookish meanderings as the translator of a marvelous collection of South Indian bhakti (devotional) poems, *When God Is a Customer*. These poems, or padams, were written, usually by men, in the voice of a woman to her lover, who is a god. Ramanujan became an inner companion and helper in a personal passion of mine—the erotic as sacred. I did not know he was a distinguished linguist and folklorist, or that he taught at the University of Chicago during the years my father taught there, until I began working on this essay.

## Me and My India

*Amaji, old mother*
*which of us swallowed the other?*[12]

I want to tell you another story, the story of me and my India. In the long ago and faraway time we call the sixties, when I was a very young woman, a twist of fate took me to India. I found myself in a culture in which the goddess was alive and still worshipped. But she was no sweet-faced Madonna. She was the dark goddess, Kali, who brings you into this life, nurses you, and chops off your head to add to her necklace of

---

11  Ramanujan, *Collected Poems*, p. 196, Stanzas 2, 3 & 4.
12  Lowinsky, "we return to mother india," *red clay is talking*, p. 68.

skulls—all in one fell swoop. She was Parvati of the voluptuous breasts and hips. She was Shakti, winding her leg around Shiva as they stood in blatant sexual embrace. She went back to the beginning of time—fierce, lusty, magical. She struck the same unstruck strings in me as did the Queen of the Night.

And yet, India was more overtly misogynist than my own culture. Indians preferred sons, abused brides, cast out widows. I learned that when a woman marries in India, she is more intricately bonded to her mother-in-law and sisters-in-law than to her own husband. It is the women of the family who create her fate and color the nature of her days. Even so, I met women in India who carried themselves with an authority and unembarrassed competence that I had not yet experienced in my own culture—doctors and lawyers who hitched up their saris and did their work with pride. These were middleclass women.

Among the poor, I met stone-carrying women, road-building women, house-building women, street-sweeping women who wore flowers in their hair. Indian women of all castes moved sinuously in their vivid saris, painted floral designs in red henna on the palms of their hands and the soles of their feet. They created intricate designs of colored sand at the doorways of their houses. They wove garlands of flowers and threw them over the heads of arriving guests. This careful attention to liminal space, to doorways, to arrivals and departures, brought another dimension to my life. One could call it mindfulness. One could call it ritual magic.

India confused me. India scared me. India enchanted me. India seduced me. India cracked open my narrow worldview, fed me bits of her ancient culture, initiated me into the wisdom of the dark feminine. Before I'd ever read Jung, India made a Jungian of me. One of India's daughters, Shanti, became my daughter. Her birth people came from a land not far from Kumudha's. Here's what I wrote in a poem about Mother India:

> amaji
> old mother...
>
> what do your dark eyes remember of me

who came to you young
full of milk and children
drunk on the manifestation of things
you taught me your dance
with naked feet slapping the heat of the earth
you taught me to carry my baby on my hip
to wrap my sari low and tight
to pound cumin seed on a stone
to cook red chillis in hot oil
until the smell comes…

amaji
old mother
which one of us swallowed the other?
did you enter my bloodstream
feed essence of rasa through me to your daughter…

did you crack my skull open
like a betel nut
chewing the west of me
in your red stained teeth and spitting out
the shells[13]

Did my early enchantment with the Queen of the Night portend my encounter with India and her goddesses? Did Ramanujan's entry into my internal world portend the path that has led me to respond to *A Flowering Tree?* Let's turn to the story within all these stories, the story of Kumudha and her prince.

## In the Mother Tongue

> …*a woman's creativity, her agency…is bound up with her capacity for speech.*[14]

As the music ushers us in to this fairytale realm, we feel an undertow of dread, of dissonance, of worlds out of kilter. The trouble is stated simply

---

13 Lowinsky, "we return to mother india," *red clay is talking*, pp. 68-69.
14 Ramanujan, *Collected Essays*, p. 413.

by the storyteller, who describes the "selfish spoiled young man," the prince, who lives in "comfort and luxury" and seldom leaves the palace "for the world outside/was a place of misery and suffering."[15] There's a moral problem in this fairytale world.

When we first meet Kumudha, she is worrying about her mother, who taught her the morning and evening prayers, who gave her and her sister life, sweet milk, and who is now struggling to survive and to feed her daughters. It is the essence of Kumudha's nature, to speak first of the spiritual practices her mother taught her. For above all, Kumudha exemplifies the religious attitude. She sings:

> If only I could become a flowering tree,
> rain down upon your thin grey hair
> cool white blossoms,
> with scent of lemon and jasmine!…
> my body a trunk
> of dark glistening bark,
> my head a crown of smooth white petals,
> my flesh the white meat of the coconut,
> my face the white of a cumulus cloud,
> joyously welcomed, long-awaited
> messenger of the coming monsoon.[16]

I remember the hot muggy air, the sweltering days of June, the air so thick you could hardly breathe it, and then, like magic that transforms the world, the monsoon, the warm gracious rains that washed away all that heavy air, that inertia. My son, then a little boy of four or five, would run out into the pouring rain, his face turned up like a thirsty flower, his hands outstretched as though invoking the gods of rain.

The evocation of the monsoon speaks to an experience every Indian has, of the transformation of the world when the rains come. Transformation happens in *A Flowering Tree* on so many levels. That is the beauty of this opera. It happens in the very language of Kumudha, who

---

15  Libretto by John Adams and Peter Sellars, *A Flowering Tree*.
16  Libretto by Adams and Sellars. *A Flowering Tree*, Act I, Scene 1.

begins with "if only" and in the way of magic turns it into an evocation of her tree self. She transforms herself with her sister's help, with meditation, ritual magic, and song. As in the ritual of the mass, she transforms herself into food (white meat of the coconut.) In a prayer taken directly from the Hindu bhakti tradition of poetry, as translated by Ramanujan, she evokes the god of the forest: "O lord white as jasmine.../ why don't you/ show me your face?" Transformation happens in the music. What has been pressured, troubled, and full of strife, opens up. The music becomes magical; there are mysterious sounds in the strings and in the chorus; there is a poignant, yearning melody.

Kumudha sees the desperate situation her mother is in, trying to support her sister and herself with no male help. She does not bemoan her fate. She does not weep and wail. She is clear as a bell. She has the audacity, the clarity, the creative imagination to make something out of nothing. She descends into some deep source within herself, the kind of source that reaches down into the realm of the dark goddess, the realm that the roots of a tree reach into to find water and nourishment from the depths of Mother Earth. Like the high priestess, she instructs her sister to pour water over her body while she sits in meditation under a tree, as did the Buddha. But unlike the Buddha, she is not releasing herself from the cycles of birth and death; she is transforming herself into one of the goddess' many life-giving forms—a flowering tree. She is not in pursuit of transcendence; she is about immanence, providing for those she loves, making her way into the world, into the marketplace with the abundance of her creativity. Hers is the ancient wisdom of India—long ago buried seeds of the dark feminine.

Kumudha has transformed her family life and her own fate. There is money now, and a prince wants her hand. That her mother misunderstands, thinks she must have prostituted herself and beats her and her sister, is part of the dark truth of this tale. It is a familiar story of mothers who've had to narrow their lives, cut off their creative gifts, deny their sensuality, deny the power of the goddess. If a daughter is admired and desired by a prince, it cannot be because she has deep wisdom and the capacity to transform herself. If a daughter finds her way into the marketplace, brings home money, it cannot be that she is clever and has found a way to use her native gifts to create saleable commodities such as flower garlands; she must be selling her body. Kumudha's mother lives partly in the patriarchal world in which women have lost their deep authority and their connection to the divine. And yet, when her daughters tell her their truth, she believes them and is grateful for what they have done for her. Their action redeems the mother, and she is returned to a world in which the feminine is magical, and daughters are precious.

The irony is, though Kumudha did not prostitute herself at the beginning of the story, she is forced to, as the story continues. The prince won't consummate their marriage until she does her flowering tree trick for him. He does not want her in her ordinary woman form, though she says to him: "I am no demon, no goddess, I am an ordinary woman." The prince wants only her magic, her shape-shifting. The storyteller sings:

> The bride sunk her face
> in the end of her sari…
> She would do what he wanted.[17]

She is held hostage to his "careless and cruel ways."

Though Kumudha suffers from the arrogance of the prince, she suffers even more terribly from the heedlessness of women. The Prince's envious sister and her friends in the orchard want to see this trick she does. But they don't honor her ritual. They don't pour enough water on her to bring her back to her woman form. They are careless, mindless. She is left half woman, half tree, stunted, a handless, footless maiden with a lovely face and beautiful singing voice, and a stump for a body. A thing. An object. A beggar. Saved from oblivion by the random care of poor folk.

> Neither tree or princess
> neither tree or loving wife
> a stump of flesh, a shapeless thing
> a twisted, mutilated body
> with neither hands nor feet…

---

17   Libretto by Adams and Sellars, *A Flowering Tree*, Act I, Scene 4.

a wounded carcass.[18]

Where is Kumudha's amazing capacity for ritual magic, for transformation, now when she needs it the most? Like the handless maiden in our European folktale, she is unable to grasp her own fate. But her fate is worse than the handless maiden's because she is footless as well, unable to stand on her own two feet. And what of our Prince, who had been loved and spoiled by his doting parents, protected from the suffering world outside the palace. He had not had to struggle or to work, he had only had to tell the King, his father, of his attraction to the magical girl to be given his heart's desire. There is something hauntingly impressive about the chorus, which shape-shifts from common people in the market to prophetic voices and confronters of the Prince. In this last role, they are merciless.

> Riding rutting elephants
> of pride, you turned easy target
> of fate.
> You qualified for hell.[19]

And hell it is for him, bereft of his love and her glorious flowering, hit by an unexpected fate that knocks him off his certainties and entitlements, and leaves him wandering, grieving, an ascetic with his begging bowl. He has become a beggar like she is.

## The Mindful Beggar

> *She who was neither cultured nor lovely,*
> *She who was filthy in disarrayed clothes,*
> *She of the lowest of castes...*[20]

---

18  Libretto by Adams and Sellars *A Flowering Tree*, Act II.
19  Libretto by Adams and Sellars, *A Flowering Tree*, Act II.
20  Mirabai, translated by Jane Hirshfield, *Women in Praise of the Sacred*, p. 135.

Beggars are central to this tale, and beggars taught me much about life when I was in India. They demonstrated resilience and creative resourcefulness in the most difficult of circumstances. There were bands of beggars in the town I lived in. Most of them suffered some sort of deformity. Some, I learned, were born that way. Others, sold by impoverished parents, were deformed on purpose, so they could command more money as beggars. I have never forgotten the king of the beggars, who had the best territory downtown, wore polyester shirts (a high status symbol), had tiny stumps for legs and arms, and a beautiful smile. He made my young children laugh as they sat in the car, by leaping up and down on his stumps, appearing and disappearing in the car windows. He proposed a deal. I would pay him 5 rupees (pennies to me, a handsome sum to him) for minding my children while I went into the store to buy what I needed. So it was that the king of the beggars became my babysitter.

It is beggars who save Kumudha. She who had been a princess was now one of them. The storyteller sings:

> Beggars in the street, themselves misshapen,
> would pick up her stump of a body
> and carry her, a freak,
> from town to town
> where she would sing sad songs
> in her clear and beautiful voice.[21]

It is the women servants of the prince's envious sister, now a queen, who see Kumudha and recognize that there is something numinous about her: "She glows like a King's daughter." The queen allows her maids to tend "the thing." They bathe her in oils, apply medicine to her wounds. They can make her well, "but they cannot make her whole."[22] The element that is necessary for healing is mindfulness. The maids are mindful. The girls in the orchard were mindless. The maids, who are servants, who are not owners of property, who have no worldly power, have the power of real sight, of deep vision. They recognize "It." They

---

21 Libretto by Adams and Sellars, *A Flowering Tree*, Act II.
22 Ramanujan, *A Flowering Tree and Other Tales*, p. 60.

bring "It" to the prince, who, in the manner of folktales, has found his way to the palace of the Queen, his sister. As Ramanujan tells it:

> With the permission of the disgusted queen, they left 'It' on his bed. He neither looked up nor said anything. But this night, 'It' pressed and massaged his legs with its stump of an arm. 'It' moaned strangely. He got up once and looked at 'It.' 'It' was sitting at his feet. He stared at 'It' for a few moments and then realized 'It' was really his lost wife. She who had had no language broke into words. She told him whose daughter she was, whose wife, and what had happened to her.[23]

When she touches the prince with her stump of an arm, he does not push her away. In a society where the touch of an untouchable is an abomination, he lets the handless maiden massage him. Because he has suffered and his ego has been deflated, he has the power of deep vision. Because he is present, mindful, and devoted, he can see who she is. And because he hears her, she regains her magical powers. She tells him the ritual he must perform. He must bring two pitchers of water, as Ramanujan tells it. He must not touch the water with his fingernails. She knows the chants she must say over the water, knows she must return to her woman form, that he must set right her broken branches, mend her torn leaves, and when her tree form is healed and whole, he must mindfully pour a second pitcher of water so she can become a whole human being again.

The elements that are necessary for wholeness then are humility, bhakti, and, as Ramanujan tells us, female agency—Kumudha's capacity to tell the prince her whole story and to be heard by him.[24] Ramanujan refers to the eloquent tradition of women poets in the bhakti tradition as an example of this agency. And he quotes Kabir, the fifteenth-century bhakti poet, who says: " 'Sanskrit is as the water of a well, but the vernacular is like a running brook.' Bhakti was a return to the language of daily speech and to the unmediated vision." Folktales, Ramanujan

---

23 Ramanujan, *A Flowering Tree*, p. 51.
24 Ramanujan, *A Flowering Tree*, p. 234.

goes on to say, often give agency to women, speaking in their mother tongues, because they give voice to the powerless.[25]

## Maya and the Holy Tree

> *So Maya, when her hour was come, bore*
> *her child beneath the plaksa tree, which*
> *bowed its crown shelteringly to earth.*[26]

How do we understand the vision in *A Flowering Tree* of kinship between woman and tree? Ramanujan gives us an example of how this story resonates with other South Indian lore. He quotes a classical Tamil poem in which Mother says that the laurel tree "qualifies/as a sister."[27]

In Sanskrit and Tamil, Ramanujan informs us, the words for flowering and for menstruation are the same. He writes: "A tree that has come to flower or fruit will not be cut down; it is treated as a mother, a woman who has given birth."[28] Jung writes: "As the seat of transformation and renewal, the tree has a feminine and maternal significance."[29] I knew none of this when I named a daughter Tamar, which means date palm. Years later, I learned that the date palm was a symbol of the Hebrew goddess Asherah, a Babylonian goddess who made her way into early Judaism. This meaning wove itself into a poem I wrote when my daughter's second child became seriously ill in his first weeks of life:

## Tamar

> Tamar is a calm palm     a swaying tree
> with salt in her roots     she sings
> her milky mother's song
>
> for her baby is sick     as is the baby

---

25 Ramanujan, *Collected Essays*, pp. 330, 469.
26 Jung, "The Type Problem in Poetry," *CW* 6, ¶ 298.
27 Ramanujan, *A Flowering Tree*, p. 219.
28 Ramanujan, *A Flowering Tree*, p. 221.
29 Jung, "The Philosophical Tree," *CW* 13, ¶ 419.

of the sad Maria     who croons in Spanish
to her fragile newborn     among

beeps and jagged graphs displaying
oxygen saturation & heart rate     Tamar sings
queen palm among the vital signs

and hospital machinery     she untangles wires
to her baby's toes and her milk flows     even here
in the dark ward     with flowered curtains

and tiny cribs so near the ocean     where the soil
is full of salt     my daughter holds her baby
in a swaying dance and sings

and  I can see     though my daughter is beyond
exhaustion     she has found her roots
that go down below down     to the mother

goddess of the palm tree out of Babylon
(smuggled into the Hebrew testament)
for whom I named her[30]

The archetypal connection between tree and woman revealed itself in other writings. Jung reminds us that according to the Koran, Mary gave birth under a palm and adds that, "Maya at the birth of the Buddha was shaded by the holy tree."[31] Jung's writings resound with many unstruck strings from long ago. In "The Philosophical Tree," he takes a meander through alchemical writings to explore the spontaneous creative expression of his patients, who kept bringing him images of trees. He brings us back to the world of the Middle Ages when a human being was seen "as a tree standing upside down, for what in the one is the root, trunk and leaves, in the other is the head and the rest of the body with the arms and feet."[32] Jung, who leaps about as freely as does the Queen of the Night, leaps from this quote to the Bhagavad Gita, where it is written:

    There is a fig tree

---

30  Lowinsky, *adagio & lamentation*, p. 86.
31  Jung, "The Philosophical Tree," *CW* 13, ¶ 418.
32  Jung, "The Philosophical Tree," *CW* 13, ¶ 412.

> In ancient story,
> The giant Ashvattha,
> The everlasting,
>
> Rooted in heaven,
> Its branches earthward;
> Each of its leaves
> Is a song of the Vedas, And he who knows it
> Knows all the Vedas.[33]

We know this tree, do we not? It resounds with the imagery of the Tree of Life, the central image in the Kabbalah, a tree whose roots reach into the heavens, whose branches reach down to the earth, whose blossoms are the ten sephirot that describe the movement and transformation of divine energy into the realm of manifestation, the realm of the feminine, of the Shekinah who is also called "Apple Orchard." Or perhaps it is the tree in the Garden of Eden. Jung writes: "In East and West alike, the tree symbolizes a living process as well as a process of enlightenment, which, though it may be grasped by the intellect, should not be confused with it."[34]

## A Thousand Year Old Oak

> *Sometimes the tree is small and young…sometimes large and old, taking the form of an oak or the world tree, in so far as it bears the sun and the moon as its fruits.*[35]

So how are we to make meaning of this, that this simple folktale told by women in South India to A.K. Ramanujan, should shape-shift with the mindful magic of John Adams and Peter Sellars into an opera performed in Europe and America? What does it mean that these two creative men have moved from the guilt and agony of *Dr. Atomic*, from the "father stories" of presidents and kings, to the "mother story" of *A Flowering*

---

33 Jung, "The Philosophical Tree," *CW* 13, ¶ 412.
34 Jung, "The Philosophical Tree," *CW* 13, ¶ 413.
35 Jung, "The Philosophical Tree," *CW* 13, ¶ 405.

*Tree?* Jung recognized the guilt of Faust who had burned down the home of the loving old couple, Baucis and Philemon, to get them out of the way of his greed, in Goethe's great drama. (In the Greek myth, Baucis and Philemon were transformed into intertwined trees.) Jung, says Edward Edinger, takes upon himself "the guilt that Faust evaded."[36] Over the entrance to his home at Bollingen, he carved the inscription: "Philemonis Sacrum—Fausti Poenitentia: Shrine of Philemon—Repentance of Faust." We who live in this richest of countries, carry Oppenheimer's guilt, Faust's guilt, the guilt of the prince and his "rutting elephants of pride," the guilt of a war-mongering superpower toward those it invades and abuses, the guilt of our own mindless consumption of oil and consumer goods, the guilt we bear the sacred earth that we have turned into a thing.

The Kabbalists understood that it was our spiritual work to heal the world; they called it "Tikkun Olam." *A Flowering Tree* gives us a vision of that healing. We must, like Kumudha, return to our tree consciousness. Like Kumudha, we must develop our spiritual imagination, our capacity for mindfulness, for bhakti. It is our spiritual work to mend the broken branches and torn leaves of the world tree.

In reflecting on the tree, I remembered the beautiful poem by Rabindranath Tagore, which states in such a clear way the Hindu view of the interconnection of things:

> The same stream of life that runs through my veins night and day runs through the world and dances in rhythmic measures.
>
> It is the same life that shoots in joy through the dust of the earth in numberless blades of grass and breaks into tumultuous waves of leaves and flowers.[37]

In reflecting on the tree, I was reminded of the magic flute, which we are told by Pamina, daughter of the Queen of the Night, was cut by her father from "the deepest roots of a thousand year old oak."[38]

---

36 Edward Edinger, *Goethe's Faust*, p. 84.
37 Rabindranath Tagore, *Gitanjali*, 1992 #69.
38 *The Magic Flute*. Libretto by Emanuel Schikaneder.

*A Flowering Tree* gives us an ancient story in a powerful musical form to illuminate our current dilemmas. We can hear Kumudha's story as a story about our relationship, or lack of it, to the deep feminine, our Mother Earth, our tree consciousness. For like the mindless girls in the orchard, we have broken Her, defiled Her, turned Her into a stump of a thing, clear-cut Her, strip-mined Her holy mountains, desecrated Her flowering trees. We can hear Her story as giving us hope for the earth's healing, for our own wholeness. Maybe that hope does not come from the great and the powerful, from presidents and senators, but from the ordinary folk who live in the mother world, creative souls such as Wangari Muta of Kenya, who won the Nobel Peace Prize in 2004 for her work organizing women to plant trees. Wangari, like Kumudha, understands that to heal ourselves, to heal our earth, we need to return to tree consciousness. We need to set right the broken branches and the torn leaves. We need to perform a ritual magic, a mindful devotional practice, to bring back our flowering nature. We must mourn what has been cut down, mourn the ancient forests.

Some years ago, a tree was cut down behind the San Francisco Institute. It was an old pine that had lived there much longer than we had. Many of us knew that tree. Baruch Gould, then our Director of Public Programs, spoke of looking out of his office and watching all the wild life in it. He could not bear to be at work the day they cut it down. He spoke of the terrible emptiness it left—a void in the air, a blankness, a dead space. On Earth Day that year, a small group of us gathered to sanctify that tree stump, to make it an altar. We made prayer flags. We wrote messages. We decorated the tree stump with stones and clay figures and leaves. We prayed over it. We danced, we rattled, we drummed, we chanted, we entered tree consciousness. The wind spoke to us. I'm sure Kumudha was with us, though I did not yet know her name.

Trees connect us to what is below, in the dark, in the underworld, in the groundwater, in the mulch and the minerals, and to what is above, in the heavens, in the winds, in the night skies. Trees transform our exhalations, our used air, into fresh air. Trees sanctify and beautify our worlds, harbor birds and squirrels, feed us their fruit, offer us their flowers to wear in our hair. The terrible secret in both *The Magic Flute* and in *A Flowering Tree* is that like the prince, we need to suffer an ordeal, undergo a dread initiation, "walk, by the power of music/ in joy through death's dark night."[39] Our narrow worldviews need to be cracked open. We need to lose our sense of entitlement. May "music protect us" in flood and in fire.

---

39  Libretto by Schikaneder, *The Magic Flute*.

# SECTION TWO

# IN THE DARK OF THE ENIGMA

## Chapter 3

## Getting the Word from Within[1]

*In the dark of the enigma the psyche gazes at herself*[2]

## What the Dream Said

> *The alchemists understood the return to chaos as an essential part of the opus.*[3]

The "Word from Within" came in a dream as I approached the end of my second Jungian analysis. I was informed that it was time for me to read Jung's *Mysterium Coniunctionis*. This message was delivered by an unshaven character, one of a group of men in a garage. They were gathered around a fire, like a welder's fire, or a blacksmith's fire. They were grubby looking and rough, had black dirt under their nails and smelt of automobile oil. What were a bunch of blue-collar types doing telling me I had to read *Mysterium*? Edinger says: "Mysterium is like the psyche itself. It's oceanic and to take it seriously means to run the

---

1 Lowinsky, published in an earlier version in *The San Francisco Jung Institute Library Journal* (now the *Jung Journal*), Vol. 24, Number 3, 2005 under the title, "After Termination: Cultivating the Other Within."
2 Jung, "The Paradoxa," *CW* 14, ¶ 93.
3 Jung, "The Personification of the Opposites," *CW* 14, ¶ 253.

risk of drowning."[4] Why, after all the work of two long analyses would I want to take that risk? And anyway, alchemy had never spoken to me. It struck me as a kind of womb envy: all those old men sitting around trying to create transformations in a vessel, the kind any woman in her reproductive years could perform without thinking about it. Of course, at the time of the dream I was long past that phase…

The men in the garage around the fire were connected to an earlier dream image—a dream I had before my first session with Joe Henderson, a founding member of the San Francisco Institute who became my mentor. In the dream, Joe showed me his collection of books, and he showed me a stove. He called it a "funda" and said it got its heat from the center of the earth. When in real life I told Joe this dream, he leapt up—to my alarm, he was in his 80s then—and pulled down a book from his shelf, which was indeed, full of books. It was Jung's *Psychology and Alchemy*,[5] and in it he showed me the image of a rough looking half-naked man stoking a fire in a furnace—a character much like the ones in my dream years later—while a group of well-dressed scholars stood about in a library. The dream word "funda" for the stove in the dream, is associated etymologically both with fundamental, meaning foundational, and with fundus, meaning womb. So the dream put together alchemy and the womb, before I was ready to, and announced that my work with Joe would provide the vessel for a fire that comes from the center of the earth, which indeed, it has. I was given an image and a magic word for my lifelong project of bringing my passion and book-learning together. That unkempt earthy animus shows up from time to time to remind me of the task.

## The Forgotten Feminine

> *The Shulamite, the priestess of Ishtar, signifies earth, nature, fertility, everything that flourishes under the damp light of the moon, and also the life urge.*[6]

---

4 Edinger, *The Mysterium Lectures*, p. 17.
5 Jung, "The Work," *CW* 12, Illustration 144.
6 Jung, "Adam and Eve," *CW* 14, ¶ 646.

The original "Word from Within" goes back over forty years to when I was a young woman, lost in life and disconnected from myself. I stumbled, fortuitously, into a Jungian symposium called, "The Forgotten Feminine." I had no idea what that meant when I signed up. The words tugged at me. I heard the San Francisco analysts Kay Bradway and Elizabeth Osterman talk about their patients, women whose creativity was blocked. In analysis they began painting or writing or dancing. It was suddenly clear to me that I was in desperate need of a Jungian analysis.

At the time, I was, to borrow Janine Auger's phrase, a "boundariless soul" who needed the help of the analyst to create a separation between me and the world at large.[7] I was a permeable membrane picking up all the moods and projections around me. I was in what Jung calls "a primitive consciousness which is constantly liable to break up into individual affective processes."[8] In my "confusion and lostness,"...I needed—to quote Jung again from *Mysterium*—"the analysis and interpretation of dreams (to) confront the conscious standpoint with the statements of the unconscious, thus widening its narrow horizon...(and allowing) a loosening up of cramped and rigid attitudes."[9] Or, to put it another way, I had to listen to the strangers in my unconscious, such as those grizzled guys in the garage—they hold the key to the mysteries.

I learned in that first analysis that the "forgotten feminine" was within me. I needed to dig down to retrieve my essential nature, which had been badly repressed both in the dynamics of my family of origin, and in a collective consciousness which had buried the goddess for thousands of years, demonized what lay below the earth, and denied the power of the moon, which, in Jung's words, "stands on the borderline between the eternal, aethereal things and the ephemeral phenomena of the earthly sublunar realm."[10]

I also learned in that analysis, which was with a man, that I needed help with my solar nature. I was scared of life. I hid out behind husband and children and feelings of inadequacy. I needed to form an ego that

---

7 *The Journal of Analytical Psychology*, Vol. 31, 1986, pp. 45-46.
8 Jung, "The Conjunction," *CW* 14, ¶ 657.
9 Jung, "The Personification of the Opposites," *CW* 14, ¶ 306.
10 Jung, "The Personification of the Opposites," *CW* 14, ¶ 173.

could bring head and body together. I needed to learn to function in the world—earn a living, write checks, pay taxes. I needed a sun nature that could relate to my moon nature, access in Jung's alchemical language to "the fruit of the sun-and-moon tree, gold and silver, or the reborn and sublimated Sol and Luna." This, as Jung says, required "the transformation of both the unconscious and the conscious"[11] levels of the psyche.

## Tracking the Fox with Turquoise Teeth

> *It is the same thing at the beginning as at the end, it was always there and yet it appears only at the end. This thing is the self, the indescribable totality...*[12]

One has the experience in analysis, of coming again and again to what one has always known, but denied, or been afraid to admit: the truth of one's feelings, the essence of who one is; that "other" that has been denied or repressed by family or cultural taboos. I remember, early in that first analysis, coming upon Marie-Louise von Franz's description of the self in her essay in *Man and His Symbols*.[13]

> This inner center is realized in exceptionally pure, unspoiled form by the Naskapi Indians, who still exist in the forest of the Labrador Peninsula. These simple people are hunters who live in isolated family groups, so far from one another that they have not been able to evolve tribal customs or collective religious beliefs and ceremonies. In his lifelong solitude the Naskapi hunter has to rely on his own inner voices and unconscious revelations; he has no religious teachers who tell him what he should believe, no rituals, festivals, or customs to help him along. In his basic view of life, the soul of man is simply an "inner companion" whom he calls "my friend" or *Mista'peo*, meaning "Great Man." Mista'peo dwells in the heart and is immortal...

---

11  Jung, "The Personification of the Opposites," *CW* 14, ¶ 181.
12  Jung, "The Personification of the Opposites," *CW* 14, ¶ 181.
13  Marie-Louise von Franz, "The Process of Individuation," in *Man and His Symbols*, p. 161.

> Those Naskapi who pay attention to their dreams and who try to find their meaning…can enter into a deeper connection with the Great Man. He favors such people and sends them more and better dreams. Thus the major obligation of an individual Naskapi is to follow the instructions given by his dreams, and then to give permanent form to them in art.

I remember thinking, "that's my religion. That's how I want to live." But it was not so easy to get there despite being "the same thing at the beginning as at the end." I learned in this first experience of analysis that the "loosening up of cramped and rigid attitudes" of which Jung spoke, requires the shattering experience of falling apart. In my initial dream, a great fortress or castle in which I live falls down. It is unclear whether this has been caused by earthquake or by a great wind. And indeed, my fairly conventional first marriage did fall apart, and soon after, when I was a single mother with small children and no marketable skills, my psyche began to fragment. Jung says, of the earthquake:

> The earthquake sends up a dark cloud: consciousness, because of the revolution of its former standpoint, is shrouded in darkness…The widening of consciousness is at first upheaval and darkness…[14]

The world seemed to splinter into luminous pieces of experience. Words whirled in my head, synchronicities sprang up and grabbed me, a flower or a phrase in a song, or a piece of furniture could grab my attention for hours. There were moments of intense ecstasy, and times of profound confusion. I remember realizing one day that I was crawling on the wooden floors of my house, so over-stimulated was I by all this wild input. I did not know it then but I was in a state the alchemists knew well: "the dark initial state" (they) called the "chaos" or the "nigredo." In this "*massa confusa,*" Jung writes, "the elements are in conflict and repel one another, all connections are dissolved. Dissolution is the prerequisite for redemption. The celebrant of the mysteries had to suffer a figurative death in order to attain transformation."[15] There are

---

14 Jung, "The Personification of the Opposites," *CW* 14, ¶ 209.
15 Jung, "Rex and Regina," *CW* 14, ¶ 381.

many descriptions in *Mysterium* of how this transformation happens. One that I find especially beautiful is Jung's retelling from the alchemist Khunrath, the story of how the lapis is made:

> Ruach Elohim (the spirit of God) penetrated to the lowest parts and to the centre…of the virginal *massa confusa*, and scattered the sparks and rays of his fruitfulness. "Thus the form impressed itself…and the purest soul quickened and impregnated the tohu-bohu, which was without form and void."[16]

I remember the piercing white light as it hit me on that wooden floor, the ecstasy, that had as yet no legs to stand on, no ground. I remember the word eeeeeeeeeeeeemotion leaping about like a wicked sprite, full of its many meanings and sounds, unable to find a poem to express it. I was, as the word means, all stirred up, experiencing an agitation of the passions which, as the American Heritage Dictionary points out, often involves physiological changes. The word emotion comes from the latin "movere"—to move and to be moved. And I, like the word that had me in its grip, was beside myself with movement, dancing, falling to the ground, crawling on the floor. All this embodied chaos, this *massa confusa* had to do with beginning to make a connection to what was still other to me, my Self, my creative center. I began writing poetry intensely during that first analysis. But I found that the descent into the tohu bohu of a poem sent me into such fragmented states of consciousness that I could not write and also live an ordinary life.

It was to be the lapis, the treasure of my second analysis, after I had established myself as a psychotherapist, made a good, loving and intimate second marriage and was on my way to becoming an analyst, that I could sink down into the tohu bohu, write a poem, and emerge in time to make dinner. The alchemist Dorn, quoted by Jung, describes the process of bringing spirit back into matter:

> In the end it will come to pass that this earthly, spagyric birth clothes itself with heavenly nature by its ascent, and then by its descent visibly puts on the nature of the centre of

---

16  Jung, "Rex and Regina," *CW* 14, ¶ 355.

the earth, but nonetheless the nature of the heavenly centre which it acquired by the ascent is secretly preserved…This spirit becomes corporeal again…[17]

Or, as Jung puts it:

It was the freeing of the soul from the shackles of darkness, or unconsciousness; its ascent to heaven, the widening of consciousness; and finally its return to earth, to hard reality.[18]

In another passage, Jung remarks:

Ascent and descent, above and below, represent an emotional realization of opposites, and this realization gradually leads, or should lead, to their equilibrium…As Dorn interprets it, this vacillating between the opposites and being tossed back and forth means being contained *in* the opposites.[19]

Many years of analysis have born for me the fruit of the sun and moon tree. I find I can mostly tolerate being tossed back and forth in the opposites and I can come out of that back and forth with poems, the product of the transcendent function—the union of conscious and unconscious processes. It is one of the treasures of my two analyses that I have found my own way of being, my own Self. Early in my life, I thought I should be a theoretical thinker, a person with big ideas. This was what was respected in my intellectual German Jewish family. I learned what I have always known deep down, that I'm a poet, and that my gift is to bring ideas into lived, felt, personal experience in a poetic way. As Jung says: "…we cannot know a thing until we have experienced it inwardly…"[20] Like the Naskapi Indians, I have to turn that inward experience into art, into poems.

When it dawned on me that I was coming to the end of my second analysis, I realized that the process of termination is like approaching

---

17  Jung, "The Personification of the Opposites," *CW* 14, ¶ 293.
18  Jung, "The Personification of the Opposites," *CW* 14, ¶ 297.
19  Jung, "The Personification of the Opposites," *CW* 14, ¶ 296.
20  Jung, "Introduction to the Religious and Psychological Problems of Alchemy," *CW* 12, ¶ 15.

death with open eyes, as though one has the choice to die or not to die, and yet keeps walking toward it. For something momentous would die, something that has organized one's life, one's psyche, made sense of chaos, for many years. And yet one chooses this voluntary ending, this death, so that some as yet unknown stranger may live. It seemed to me a practice run for death. It is often said that facing death makes one's life pass before one's eyes in a flow of memories pervaded. I found that facing termination made a flood of images from my analyses come pouring through me; these resulted in a series of poems. Here is one:

### in her chair

> SHE    *in great heaven*
>             *turned her ear*
>             *to great earth*
>                     Enheduanna

she combs through your dreams
braids your thoughts
ties a purple ribbon in them
                    remembering pieces of how
                            you came in

                        head of a girl
                        in a tower
                              foot stamping
                                    dwarf
                your grandmother's
                      lost silver
                            hands

hour after hour she followed you
                into that storied dark
            cave eyes
                hollowed out ear
                          belly

                              tracking the fox
                                  with turquoise teeth

she was there

in her chair
when the great snake wandered away
from the center of the earth

> *your back went out*
> *there was something wrong*
> *with your guts*

she was there when the bomb blew up
in the oven
she heard the howling

she was there
when the tower fell

and when the woman in a red sari
gold coins on her belly dancer's belt
tucked you into
bed
told you
the real story[21]

The real story is what I would have to be able to hear by myself, alone, once analysis was over. Could I really do that? Perhaps you know this story in your own life. The "word from within" has been spoken by the analyst, who has stood in for angel, devil, mother, father, lover, animal soul, soothsayer, provocateur—the many unclaimed aspects of the Self. Complexes have taken over, been named, their fierce power tamed by familiarity. Dreams have been contemplated, played with, amplified—they have brought light into hitherto dark places. The relationship between you and your analyst has been strong and tumultuous. You have felt understood and sometimes misunderstood. And when that has happened you've been able to do something you could never do as a child—speak your truth and have it heard and acknowledged. The once or twice a week ritual has been a regular rhythm in your life—you depend on it, you love it.

Perhaps you wrestled with a difficult angel, who finally revealed to you the secret of your creativity. Maybe your analyst was the only one

---

21  Lowinsky, *crimes of the dreamer,* pp. 25-6.

who knew the ins and outs of the struggle, and cheered you on. Perhaps, to paraphrase Jung, it was a *longissima via*,[22] not straight but snake-like, uniting the opposites, a path whose twists and turns were not lacking in terrors. Perhaps you let yourself fall into a regressive analysis, on a couch, where your baby self, your child self was seen and heard, where you suffered old wounds and were free to express nasty, needy, shadowy feelings, even to write poems about them, for example, sometime in the middle of the work, a poem about your analyst's vacation:

### in the absence of the dream doctor

>while you were gone
>a bad mood snatched me
>I fell into a place of mud
>earth clung to me and would not let me go
>
>my heart hurt
>no one knew
>my dreams scared me
>no one knew
>a good thing happened
>no one knew
>a bad thing happened
>no one knew
>
>while you were gone
>babies were born
>people got married
>planes crashed
>the owl hooted
>a deer looked me in the eyes
>for a long moment
>one morning
>at the bottom of the hill
>
>while you were gone

---

22 Jung, "Introduction to the Religious and Psychological Problems of Alchemy," *CW* 12, ¶ 6.

that big bully girl
I've told you about
turned out to be your daughter
in a dream
you made her go away
you even made a fist at her
which was helpful
but even you don't know
what you did for me
in the dream

a little boy
had sewn himself into a pillow
he was suffocating
on goose down
swallowing chicken
feathers
until his big
red bearded brother
cut him out of there

a gnostic singer sits silent
by a huge blue glass aquarium
fish swim in it
(this happens in a dream)

while you are gone
an alchemist tells me
the treasure is in
the lower heaven
(this happens in a book)

while you are gone
red onions make
a joyful noise in my mouth
they burn in my gut
I put my ear to the belly of
the lower heaven
(this happens in my stomach)

you tell me there's a growth

in my navel
I need to have it checked out
right away
now what is that
supposed to mean
a self devouring prophesy
in the place of chi
just as I was learning
to breathe
from my belly
letting the tired old reach
for outer glory
fall away
like the long red strips
of madrone bark
under which the new baby green flesh
is revealed

what am I supposed to do
with diagnostic information
that you give me
in a dream
while you are gone

I find a red fox
in a great crowd of people
he has a small mouth
just like the dental hygienist said
I do
only his is full of
pointy turquoise teeth
I want to stroke him
he wants to bite me

he says
he is the fast and tricky run
of my mind
the leap
the play
the disappearance into
the bushes

the quick brown fox
from learning how to type
is actually red
is actually fierce
has turquoise teeth

while you are gone
he runs back into
> my woods[23]

Clearly, the attachment is strong and absence is difficult. The analyst's vacation is a foreshadowing of termination. At the time I wrote that poem, I could not conceive of choosing to end what was such an integral part of my psychological process.

## The Alchemist's Apprentice

> *Sometime he must set about the opus himself, for, as the alchemists emphasize, nobody else can do it for him.*[24]

But, things change. A time came when I yearned for a phase in my life which would be about my own connection to my gods. I was surprised by these feelings. I had often joked that I had decided to become a Jungian analyst so I could be in analysis forever. It seemed to me so rich, so essential, so life enhancing a process. Why would one give up such a treasure? Because one does not live forever, neither does one's analyst. One wants to do other things with one's time, money and psychological process. Eventually, the projections wear off and it's a colleague you're sitting with. Your dreams begin to tell you it is time. A patient who has been in analysis most of her life and has just begun imagining that she will terminate, told me a dream in which a rainbow trout leaps out of a pond in her backyard into her arms. At first, she thinks the fish is dinner. Then, she is filled with feeling for the fish, who is dying out of water, and wanders the world until she finds a vessel with fresh water

---

23 Lowinsky, *crimes of the dreamer*, pp. 21-24.
24 Jung, "The Conjunction," *CW* 14, ¶ 657.

to carry it in. I thought, what a beautiful image of the post termination process, keeping that fish alive!

My dreams kept telling me I needed alchemy to keep the fish of my soul alive. Why alchemy? Why was I being led in the direction of a strange hermetic practice having to do with turning lead into gold? Wasn't poetry my form of alchemy? Hadn't my analyses released the poet in me to play with language and make poems, transforming one state of consciousness, words and images, into another state of being? And anyway, wasn't alchemy a central metaphor for the analytic process itself? Weren't Jungians always referring to the beautiful series of images called the Rosarium, in which the King and Queen are joined in the bath, to describe the processes of transference and countertransference? In my psyche, the alchemist sat alone, engaged in strange practices, talking to inner figures. The answer came to me in reading *Mysterium*, where Jung says: (I've changed the gender pronouns in this passage, because it speaks to me so directly):

> Return to the parents has become impossible, so she hangs on to the analyst. She can go neither backwards or forwards… The analyst's guidance in helping her to understand…her unconscious…may provide the necessary insight, but when it comes to the question of real experience the analyst can no longer help her: She must put her hand to the work. She is then in the position of an alchemist's apprentice who is inducted into the teachings by the Master and learns all the tricks of the laboratory. But sometime she must set about the opus herself, for, as the alchemists emphasize, nobody else can do it for her…The light that gradually dawns on her consists in her understanding that her fantasy is a real psychic process which is happening to her personally…If you place yourself in the drama as you really are…you create…(a) rapprochement with the unconscious. This is where insight, the *unio mentalis*, begins to become real. What you are now creating is the beginning of individuation…[25]

---

25  Jung, "The Conjunction," *CW* 14, ¶ 751.

What Jung told me in that passage in *Mysterium* is that alchemy is about the creation of an ongoing dialogue with the Self, that Self I first read about in Marie-Louise von Franz's description of the Naskapi Indians, and that has become more palpable and real to me, as a lived experience, over many years of analysis. Now I needed to make it my own. Alchemy is about death and rebirth, about the spirit in matter, about falling apart and being lost in darkness, about the treasure so ordinary it is despised, and yet it transforms consciousness. I did not know when my dreams began guiding me toward alchemy, why I would need all the help from ancient practices I could find.

## What Sophia Said

> *When Sophia walks among us again, the temple of each heart will be inspirited.*[26]

A few months out of analysis, I began to flounder, things fell apart, I was in a *massa confusa*. I had not expected, after so many years of analytical containment, years of working with my dreams, doing active imagination, learning to contain intense affects, such a sense of derailment: a great grinding to a halt, a loss of inner and outer orientation. Where was I? and with whom? In analysis, one is in a regular relationship with an outside other who stands in for the Self one is just beginning to glimpse. But now, after an initial few months of well-being, I found myself in chaos, there was much clanging and groaning as I tried to hear what was within me—the voices of many internal figures, all wanting to be heard at the same time. There was a babble of dreams and poems, piles of notebooks, dreambooks, piles of books by Paracelsus, Marie-Louis von Franz, Edward Edinger, and Jung. I remembered a dream I had had shortly before my certification as a Jungian analyst, in which Jung waggled his eyebrows at me, looking for all the world like Groucho Marx. Jung the trickster was up to his old tricks, as was my psyche.

I had imagined I would leave analysis feeling whole and clear. Shortly before the end of my analysis, a dark woman had appeared to me in a

---

26 Matthews, *Sophia*, p. xxvi.

dream. She stood among other women, dignified, beautiful, feet firmly on the ground. I was being fed by the women—corn, black beans, red peppers, being prepared for a wedding. But it was the dark woman who drew my attention, she whom I engaged in active imagination. She told me her name is Sophia, spelled with a "ph" in distinction from the name Sofia I had given one of my daughters as a middle name. Her father, she said, is Greek, her mother African.

She comes from the wisdom tradition in the Bible and in Gnosticism. As I read alchemy, I found her referred to, again and again. I found a passage in von Franz, associating her with the Queen of Sheba who came from Ethiopia, and had a love affair with Solomon in the Old Testament. She represents the feminine principle, which has been so long lost to the western mind's understanding of divinity, but was kept alive in the Kabbalah, in Jewish and Christian mystical traditions, and by the alchemists. Bringing her to consciousness is what, at base, my whole analytical opus has been about. In active imagination, with me, she is at once poetic and practical, inspiring and maternal. She says:

*I am earth voice, sky voice, ocean voice, river voice, light in the leaves, night sky, day sky. I have come to your dream to tell you to guard yourself, protect your energy, speak from the earth, from the ground under your feet. I am your guide as you leave analysis.*

That seemed reassuring. I was also reassured by a dream, soon after the end of my analysis, in which a bearded man showed me his garden where grew a profusion of crystals in many glowing pastel colors. Later, in active imagination, he tells me he is Stephen Dedalus, the young writer in James Joyce's *Portrait of the Artist as a Young Man*. He says:

*I met you when you were a young woman, reading Eliot and Joyce, in love with literature and language but terrified of the artist in your self. It's taken you all these years to come back to me.*

## What the Rabbi Said

*Everything sings, celebrates, serves, develops, evolves, uplifts, aspires to be arranged in oneness.*[27]

---

27  Daniel C. Matt, *The Essential Kabbalah*, p. 153.

I was surprised and puzzled by a dream in which the Sophia figure is again preparing me for a wedding, and an ecstatic Chassidic rabbi lifts me up into the air like the bride at a Jewish wedding. He is joyful about me, celebrating my new status. What can that mean? Rabbis are foreign to me. My experience as a child and young person in synagogue was stultifying. I had a dream about a rabbi years ago, when I was beginning to speak in public about the goddess. He showed up in his black robes while I was preparing to give a talk, and raced to get to the podium before me. Then he began a dry boring sermon. I had to make a scene in public, tell him this was MY talk, shove him out of my place on the podium before I could speak from my own feminine authority. When I speak in active imagination to the Chassidic rabbi, he tells me that *Mysterium* is full of references to the Kabbalah, the mystical Jewish tradition that intertwines masculine and feminine. He says the next step on my path is to be initiated into Jewish mysticism. "Wait a moment" I say, "I'm already overwhelmed." He smiles at me, his face full of joy and light. "I know. I'm just here to remind you."

So even the dream figures contribute to my chaos. They argue with each other and with me. Sophia keeps warning me about over stimulation. She wants me to follow one thread. Stephen Dedalus isn't happy unless a poem is being made. He is always foraging about looking for new inspiration, which upsets Sophia, who wants me to calm down. The grizzled characters from the garage keep sticking their unshaven faces into my messy psyche, reminding me to read *Mysterium*. And the Chassidic rabbi is a nudge: "Don't forget about the Kabbalah!" I'm overwhelmed again, fallen back into the original tohu bohu. I wake in the night, trying to hear the dream, confused, bemused. Stephen Dedalus says: "This is what poetry is for. Write your confusion."

## I wake to question the night

> what are you stirring in me?
> some cup of zero?
> you have ladled out too many dreams
> even a sleeping bear cannot digest them

> the well dressed angel
> in a bad part of town
> says it is time
>
> someone important
> has painted a tree made of words
> whose roots go down
>               below down
>
> whose tongue is in my ear
> whose hand is shaking    my heart
>
> cradle rock me back
> to the sleep of where
>               I began
>
> be my dark
> cooking vessel
> stew for tomorrow
>
>               my bones[28]

So here I am back where I began, in a stew, deep in the tohu bohu, after most of a life of analysis! I feel like the psalmist:

> *I sink in deep mire, where there is no standing: I am come into deep waters, where the floods overflow me.*
> *I am weary of my crying: my throat is dried: mine eyes fail while I wait for my God.*[29]

## The Call of the Wild

> *Something…has stopped up the source of your fantasy, the fountain of your soul.*[30]

I have no inclination to go back into analysis. I feel I am wrestling for my own access to that "funda," the stove in my dream of Joe Hender-

---

28  Lowinsky, *crimes of the dreamer*, p. 9.
29  *King James Bible*, Psalm 69.
30  Jung, "The Personification of the Opposites," *CW* 14, ¶ 191.

son—the heat at the center of the earth. Reading *Mysterium* is a great comfort. I am carried away in a tide of images, and inspired by Jung's capacity to swim about in this ocean of texts, and bring them into a focus that holds enormous beauty and meaning for me. For example, he takes an ancient text from an alchemist named Philaletha which reads:

> If thou knowest how to moisten this dry earth with its own water, thou wilt loosen the pores of the earth, and this thief from the outside will be cast out with the workers of wickedness, and the water, by an admixture of the true Sulphur, will be cleansed from the leprous filth and from the superfluous dropsical fluid...[31]

Jung translates this arcane recipe into a psychological challenge:

> If you will contemplate your lack of fantasy, of inspiration and inner aliveness, which you feel as sheer stagnation and a barren wilderness, and impregnate it with the interest born of alarm at your inner death, then something can take shape in you, for your inner emptiness conceals just as great a fullness if only you will allow it to penetrate into you. If you prove receptive to this "call of the wild," the longing for fulfillment will quicken the sterile wilderness of your soul as rain quickens dry earth.[32]

I don't know what Philaletha would have made of Jung's amplification of his text. But both the text and Jung's interpretation speak to me. I feel the roots of a lineage through Jung that goes deep into western culture, of those who struggle to be fully alive. My problem, of course, is not a lack of fantasy, but too much of it. But it does seem true to me that I needed the "call of the wild," my own deepest instincts, and water to nourish my earth.

The call of the wild in me whispers, is it Sophia?—"the way you get through things is to wrestle with them in writing. So," she says, "give yourself the task of writing about termination, about alchemy, about wrestling with the stranger within. Use your readings in alchemy to flesh

---

31  Jung, "The Personification of the Opposites," *CW* 14, ¶¶ 189-191.
32  Jung, "The Personification of the Opposites," *CW* 14, ¶ 190.

it out." Sounds good, even easy. My mood improves. It helps to have a project. It is like a cry from my soul. I give my essay an epigram from *Mysterium,* which seems to me to sum up the whole process: "in the dark of the enigma the psyche gazes at herself."

But as I begin to approach the actual writing, all hell breaks out again. I am overwhelmed. I have many notebooks of marvelous passages I've gleaned from Jung, Edinger, von Franz, Paracelsus, and a book on the Alchemical Imagination by Jeffrey Raff. I have piles of poems that came out of my termination. I have notebooks full of dreams before and after termination. But I have no idea how to organize it. It feels oceanic, as Edinger says of *Mysterium,* like trying to hold the ocean in a small vessel. Raff writes: "We might imagine the psyche as a chaotic place, in which every part is capable of generating its own image. With every aspect of the inner world able to personify itself as an image, the result would be a conflicting chorus of voices, each singing its own melody, with no regard for the others… Balancing this disorder, however, is the self, the principle of order and harmony."[33]

So, where is my Self? Who is going to organize this paper? Raff describes the "religious attitude as paying attention to the self…making it into an inner partner."[34] I know this. And I know, to borrow Jung's words, that the "fiery parts of the world soul were already in the chaos, the prima materia, at the beginning of the world."[35] I have copied down many times Jung's quote from the early Christian theologian, Origen—"I am scattered in all things…in gathering me thou gatherest together thyself."[36] That's what I am trying to do, to gather myself, in several senses of the word—gathering as in bringing together, harvesting, and understanding. But who is to do the gathering? The Self is in pieces.

And suddenly, Sophia appears to me. She is laughing at me. *So,* she says, *you've noticed that you don't have a monotheistic self. That is something you've paid lip service to, but now you are suffering the actual experience of many gods fighting for your attention. Your conflict is the whole point. You*

---

33 Raff, *Jung and the Alchemical Imagination,* p. 8.
34 Raff, *Jung and the Alchemical Imagination,* p. 19.
35 Jung, "The Paradoxa," *CW* 14, ¶ 50.
36 Jung, "The Components of the Coniunctio," *CW* 14, note 26.

remember what von Franz said about this in her *Alchemy* book. You wrote it down in one of your many notebooks:

> The only way the Self can manifest is through conflict: to meet one's insoluble and eternal conflict is to meet God… That is the moment of surrender…If you let yourself be torn in the conflict, then suddenly you change, you change from the deepest root of your being and the whole thing has another aspect.[37]

It is suddenly clear to me that writing this essay is an alchemical process. It is the vessel in which I'll cook all this prima materia—my way of making my own connection to the Self. Of course I have to begin in this chaos of books, dreams, poems, and the detritus of a head cold. There is no analyst to bring this to, no warm concerned presence sitting in the other chair. No eyes to see what I'm not seeing. No voice to guide me through this mess, keep the faith, help me pick my way through the dark into the light. There is just me, and all these characters inside me. This is the whole point—I was, am, will be, on my own. Great! And an essay to complete. What if I just stay in this nigredo. What if chaos never lifts? What then?

## Like the First Snake

> *The Serpent serves as metaphor for the impenetrable manner in which our lives change, twist and renew themselves.*[38]

At this point, Stephen Dedalus steps in, reminding me that the lapis of my analytic work is my poetry. All I have to do to organize my essay is to gather some of my poems about ending analysis—make a narrative of them. The poems will get at the shifting, meandering "word from within." He reminds me that I have written a poem about the sinuous serpentine path that makes connections between numinous fragments of experience. It's called "snake and stone story." It's dedicated to Betty

---

37  von Franz, *Alchemy*, p. 137.
38  Johnson, *Lady of the Beasts*, p. 128.

Meador, whose wonderful translation from Enheduanna provides me with the epigraph, and inspiration.

## snake and stone story

*for Betty*

*like the FIRST SNAKE*
*i come out of the mountains*
    Enheduanna

the story is
        unutterable
        magnetic

comes down from the mountains
    arises from the center of the earth
tugs at the soles of my feet
from under the stones at santa croce
    from the roots of the willow at river's edge

    from the base of my spine to the tip of the old
            snake brain
            swan's neck arches

snake glides through the whole
meander    ties it all together like the needle pulls the thread
    only I can't see the gleaming point

    why do you speak to me in mysteries?

    unspeakable mouth of the underworld
        tell me your stone stories
        what got burned
        what broken
        into a thousand pieces
            casting out

the whole howling sacred circle—oak tree   blue stone   sun cycle
        dark of the moon
I want my grandmother's loch ness treasure    her basket of snakes
        her sea chest    engraved with

> your old wild
> name[39]

Sophia comments: *This is a poem about Great Snake, who has come to you again and again, in dream and in imagination. Snake is the mysterious magnetism of your own life unfolding, as you felt the earth magnetism when you were at Avebury in England. Do you remember? You stood and leaned your head against a standing stone in the ancient circle. You heard the howling.*

Stephen Dedalus suggests the next poem, one that deals directly with the theme of ending analysis:

## when my song breaks loose

will it all come back to me
what was mine before

> I was

> the spindle

I gave you to hold
the long story told

> in dreams
> while you sat
> with your ear
> to the sound within sound
> that was my
> > lost voice

> yours my eye
> > for the silver gleam
> yours my nose
> > for the fishy
> yours my grasp
> > for who visited nights
> > > yellow tiger
> > > green snake
> even yours
> > the hot salt of tears

---

39  Lowinsky, *crimes of the dreamer*, p. 57.

>                             so I wonder
>     when we two cease our infinity
>                     loop of eyes
>                                 breath
>                                 heart
>
>                         will it all go flat?
>
>     will morning say nothing
>                                 to evening?
>
>     will moon lose her moorings
>
>                             will stars crash?
>
> or will sky tiger
> snake of the night forest
>         come to my bed
>         become stripe of my stripe
>                     spine of my spine?⁴⁰

## Gone the Long Story

> *Happily, nature sees to it that the unconscious contents will irrupt into consciousness sooner or later and create the necessary confusion.*⁴¹

In Janine Auger's paper on termination, she describes a kind of person for whom the "act of separation in the form of termination from analysis can be a dynamic creative act of the self which would not manifest otherwise. "For some," she writes, "…the very goal of their work is to experience an ending that is constructive and creative in…establishing their own…uniqueness and maturity."⁴² I find this a very helpful idea. But what does this "dynamic, creative act of the self" look like? The literature has much to say about what happens before the actual moment of termination. But no one writes of what happens to the solitary soul

---

40  Lowinsky, unpublished poem.
41  Jung, "The Conjunction," *CW* 14, ¶ 672.
42  *JAP*, Vol. 31, 1986, pp. 45–61.

afterwards. It's like asking the dead to speak, or the newly born. Stephen Dedalus says I'm getting off my track. My "dynamic creative act of the self" is the book of poems I wrote about analysis—*crimes of the dreamer.*

The unshaven characters in the garage are stirring. *What about Mysterium?* They wonder. *Have you forgotten Jung and Alchemy?* The Chassidic rabbi steps in: *When are you going to start reading Kabbalah? Slow down,* says Sophia. *One thing at a time. For this essay you are reading alchemy.*

I pick up Jung's *Psychology and Alchemy* and read:

> ...it seems as if all the personal entanglements and dramatic changes of fortune that make up the intensity of life were nothing but hesitations, timid shrinkings, almost like petty complications and meticulous excuses for not facing the finality of this strange and uncanny process of crystallization. Often one has the impression that the personal psyche is running around the central point like a shy animal, at once fascinated and frightened, always in flight, and yet steadily drawing nearer.[43]

The shy animal reminds Stephen Dedalus of the little red mare who showed up in a poem I wrote about ending analysis.

## ending

the hour that had been a vessel
    turned upside down
        poured itself out
           as sea salt

  the dream
  looked into her own eyes in the mirror
  over her left shoulder she saw
        a green sun setting

  we are gone
  who have been sitting here
  she in her deep chair

---

43  Jung, "The Symbols of the Self," *CW* 12, ¶ 326.

    me on her couch
           regular as clock
                    work

gone the long story
or sunk into sand
she will not know what I dream
        even if
        she's in it

on a day that could have been
a chalice or a cave
the little red mare who knew
where everything should be
        stood still and stared
        at the empty hour[44]

    The themes of loss and ending are different when the analysand is the one who choses to end the analysis, or when the analysis ends because of changes in the analyst's life, or because the analyst dies. A friend's analysis ended abruptly, traumatically, because of the sudden, unexpected death of her analyst. Her experience speaks to the synthetic function of the unconscious, how it can know things in advance we don't know we know. She told me that a few months before her analyst's death there was a rupture, a painful misunderstanding between them. She felt then as if he had died for her—her trust in him was gone. However, he and she were able to work it through. He could totally understand how he had failed her and he expressed his own pain about letting her down. This prefigured his death. She feels now that it gave her a way to work with him on her loss of him, though neither one of them knew, consciously, that it was coming. She had a dream that he and she were in a familiar safe room together. But he showed her the open door, and showed her how to build a safe staircase to take her down the hill the room was on. This dream too came before his death. And afterwards she understood it as a guiding dream, a pre-cognitive dream. He was showing her the door out of the container they shared.

---

44  Lowinsky, first published in *Edgz*.

*The unshaven characters in the garage are agitating for alchemy. Stop listening to Stephen Dedalus and listen to Jung, they tell me. Your Stephen Dedalus just wants to bring in as many poems as he can. But you know your real job is to become the alchemist's apprentice. The alchemists used meditation, meditatio, to mean when one "has an inner dialogue with someone unseen....with God ...or with (one's) good angel."⁴⁵ Jung speaks of this as a living relationship to the answering voice of the "other." You need to meditate upon the alchemist in your soul!*

## What the Alchemist Said

> *In order to acquire the "golden understanding" one must keep the eyes of the mind and soul well open, observing and contemplating by means of that inner light which God has lit in nature and in our hearts from the beginning.*⁴⁶

"Is there an alchemist in my soul?" I wonder.

*Yes!* The answer is rapid, the speaker is clear in my inner eye. He is a small, dark complexioned man from Southern Europe. He could be a Spaniard, a Moor. I know who he is. He showed up in a dream, about a month after the end of my analysis. He was on a secret mission, had to hole up in some woman's apartment. I brought him a child for safekeeping. I never understood that dream. Now I get it—the secret mission has to do with alchemy. The child, of course, is the analytic child who needs someone to care for her. He says:

*Yes, I am he who came to you in a dream. I come from the 12th century, also the 9th, the 1st, and earlier, from much earlier. I have to do with secret practices, Arab manuscripts, Sufi dances, Troubadour songs, the life of the imagination, your old secret life, burning in the funda. I have a secret that has been with me since the time of the Egyptians. It is not a secret I'm going to tell for everyone must come to it in his or her own way. But you need to know it's there. I am here to guide and teach you. It has to do with knowing your deepest Self, always staying in touch with that Self you first encountered*

---

45  Jung, "Meditation and Imagination," *CW* 12, ¶ 390.
46  Jung, "The Psychic Nature of the Alchemical Work," *CW* 12, ¶ 381.

*as an idea when you read of the Naskapi Indians, that Self that brings you dreams and inner figures to talk to. I am the carrier of a tradition that goes back to Egypt.*

*Let me tell you a story about the origin of alchemy. One of the earliest alchemical texts, an old Greek one in the Codex Marianus (probably first century A.D.), entitled "The Prophetess Isis to her son" gives us a glimpse into the Egyptian tradition of alchemy. Isis writes a letter to her son Horus, telling him about her experience with the angel Amnael, who came to earth full of desire for her. She put him off, she writes her son, saying she wanted him to give her the secret of alchemy first. Here is part of the text:*

> I resisted him and overcame his desire till he showed me the sign on his head, and gave me the tradition of the mysteries without keeping anything back…He then again pointed to the sign, the vessel he carried on his head, and began telling the mysteries and about the message. Then he first mentioned the great oath and said: "I conjure you, in the name of Fire, of Water, of Air and of the Earth…I conjure you in the name of the Height of Heaven and the Depth of the Earth and the Underworld; I conjure you, in the name of Hermes and Anubis, the Howling of Kerkoros and the guardian dragon; I conjure you, in the name of that boat and its ferryman, Acharontos…"[47]

*Why do I tell you this story? Because I want you to know what alchemy really is. Not womb envy, but an ancient hermetic practice to protect and keep alive the secrets of the womb, the moon, and the processes of imagination that bring masculine and feminine together. I want you to understand that alchemy is a secret that Isis received because she was smart and tricky, and because an angel desired her. The angels long for us as much as we long for them. Jung writes: "It is the moral task of alchemy to bring the feminine…into harmony with the…spirit."[48] And that is the point. For it is not just the feminine, not just Sophia, or Isis, or soul, but the ancient masculine, the hairy wild man of your first analysis, that burly neanderthal type who showed up early in your second analysis, moving great rocks to create a sacred*

---

47 von Franz, *Alchemy*, p. 46.
48 Jung, "The Components of the Coniunctio," *CW* 14, ¶ 35.

*space, those alchemical characters in the garage, the half naked alchemist heating up the funda, me, the alchemist in your soul, whose company you require these days.*

*Isis received a secret recipe involving quicksilver, the mercurial substance that leaps about in the original chaos but can be transformed into the stone, the lapis. What it was in the beginning is what it is in the end—the work of the rest of your life. We never learn, from Isis, whether she ever did get it on with that angel, but we do learn, from the alchemists and from Jung, that masculine and feminine need each other, and that their joining is essential for individuation. When Amnael the angel makes his fearful oath, conjuring Isis, he does so in the name of the four elements, the three worlds, the howling Kerkoros who are spirits of death, and the ferryman Acharontos who takes dead souls across the river to the underworld. So now you are across the river, a river you never imagined you would cross, and I am your guide.*

So I do have an alchemist in my soul. I know he is speaking to me of things I don't yet understand, the coniunctio, the mysteries. But since he has spoken to me I have felt a quickening, a brightening, a feeling of subtle joy, of something opening, of something magic, like the aurora borealis I saw in a dream, at dawn, glowing in the east, filled with the stars. Is that what the alchemists call the albedo, the whitening? Since that alchemist has spoken to me I have been able to pick my way through the chaos of books and notebooks and yellow stickies and dreams, I have found the thread that I could follow through this essay. Jung describes this feeling (again, I change the gender pronouns because this passage speaks so directly to me):

> It is the state of someone who, in her wanderings among the mazes of her psychic transformation, comes upon a secret happiness which reconciles her to her apparent loneliness...In communicating with herself she finds...an inner partner;...a secret love...a hidden springtime, when the green seed sprouts from the barren earth.[49]

---

49 Jung, "Adam and Eve," *CW* 14, ¶ 623.

## comes someone's music

> *comes the unturned page comes the name comes the footstep*
> —W.S. Merwin

comes wild
   the word
      who knows who
         blew it in
            says it is
               ocean
               oars' creak
               gulls' cry
                      at sun set

comes a pulse
    knows it is someone's
        heart
        lungs
        liver
        spleen
        handclap of gypsies
        footstamp of bharat-
            natyam dancer

comes a certain music
    does not remember
        its name
        whose famous old song
            has broken
               and entered
                   this house?

        snatch of Sappho?
        murmur of psalmist?
        laughter of Miribai's lord?

comes the old story
      night ripper
      the one about
          going down

                            under
                            to visit her sister
                                        veil torn
                                        meat hook
                                        death's eye

comes long silence

            she says
            can be language

                        there's a music
                        even down here
            spirit moves
                                    shades chant
                                    in her dream
                                    someone is singing

                                                    the sun
                                                        back[50]


---

50   Lowinsky, first published in *The Ashville Poetry Review*.

# Chapter 4

## The Devil and the Deep Blue Sea: Faust as Jung's Myth and Our Own[1]

*Faust was Jung's lifelong companion.*[2]

### My Father & Jung's Mother

*You must read Goethe's Faust...*[3]

I wandered into Goethe's *Faust* some fifteen years ago and have not stopped wandering in it since. Like Jung, I think, "one cannot meditate enough about *Faust*."[4] My devotion to *Faust* came after much resistance. Who was I resisting? My father. He, who was a learned professor, who had been raised and educated in Germany, who knew *Faust* better than I knew *Hamlet*, said to me over and over again: "What kind of an education is it if you haven't read Goethe's *Faust*?" My father was pushy; my

---

1 Lowinsky, published in an earlier form in *Psychological Perspectives*, Vol. 52, Issue 2/2009.
2 Edinger, *Goethe's Faust: Notes for a Jungian Commentary*, p. 9.
3 Jung, *MDR*, p. 60. Note: *MDR* refers throughout this publication to *Memories, Dreams, Reflections*.
4 Jung, *Letters I*, p. 89.

father was domineering; my father was always right. My father was long dead before I learned how right he was.

I was preparing to teach an introductory course on Jungian Psychology when my father's ghost showed up, still ranting about Faust. Jung's mother showed up too, as she appears in *Memories, Dreams, Reflections*, telling Jung it was time he read *Faust*.[5] These two, an unlikely pair, put their heads together and came up with a plan for my class: *Faust* would provide the "basic outline and pattern," which, by the way, is precisely what Jung said *Faust* did for him.[6]

My father and Jung's mother were absolutely right. *Faust* turned out to be an excellent entryway into Jungian psychology. References to *Faust* are pervasive throughout Jung's opus. Check out **Goethe:** *Faust* in the General Index to the *Collected Works*. There are three columns with references to every volume. *Faust* provided a template, a map, for Jung's psychology. Teaching *Faust* I found that it also provided a dramatic and experiential way into such concepts as shadow, anima, libido, the descent to the underworld, alchemy and coniunctio. These concepts came alive for my students, and they could recognize them in their own lives.

*Faust* is also valuable for those of us who know Jung's ideas well. Jung, after all, is a lifelong companion to many of us. If *Faust* was his life long companion, shouldn't *Faust* be our companion too, perhaps even our kin? Remember, Jung contemplated the possibility that Goethe was his kin:

> It had been bruited about that my grandfather Jung had been an illegitimate son of Goethe's. This annoying story made an impression upon me insofar as it at once corroborated and seemed to explain my curious reactions to Faust…I was instinctively familiar with that concept which the Indians call karma.
>
> Faust struck a chord in me and pierced me through in a way that I could not but regard as personal. Most of all, it awak-

---

5 Jung, *MDR*, p. 235.
6 Jung, *MDR*, p. 235.

> ened in me the problem of opposites, of good and evil, of mind and matter, of light and darkness. Faust, the inept, purblind philosopher, encounters the dark side of his being, his sinister shadow, Mephistopheles, who in spite of his negating disposition represents the true spirit of life as against the arid scholar who hovers on the brink of suicide. My own inner contradictions appeared here in dramatized form… I was directly struck, and recognized that this was my fate.[7]

My encounter with *Faust* came much later in life than Jung's—Jung was fifteen,[8] I was pushing fifty—but something fell into place for me, and I understood why Jung considered *Faust* "the most recent pillar in that bridge of the spirit which spans the morass of world history, beginning with the Gilgamesh epic, the *I Ching*, the Upanishads…"[9] *Faust* gave me an outline, an understanding of the myth we are living.

## Goethe, Jung's Ancestor

> *I don't think Goethe was aware himself of how profoundly he was influenced by alchemy.*[10]

Goethe was born in Frankfurt am Main in 1749. There are some strong similarities in his childhood to Jung's early life and influences. Goethe's father, like Jung's, had a dry and didactic temperament. Goethe felt connected to his grandfather, who had the gift of "second sight." Goethe, like Jung, was comfortable with the occult and the irrational from childhood. In late adolescence Goethe became ill. Alice Raphael, the author of *Goethe and the Philosopher's Stone*, writes:[11]

> While physical and emotional problems contributed each their share, yet another factor in this complex situation must be reconsidered—namely, Goethe's conflict with religious

---

7  Jung, *MDR*, pp. 234-5.
8  Jung, *Letters I*, p. 88.
9  Jung, *Letters I*, p. 89.
10  Jung, *Letters I*, p. 291.
11  Raphael, *Goethe and the Philosopher's Stone*, p. 10.

authority. His inner difficulties took form at the period when he was preparing for confession in the Lutheran church his family attended. He writes... that a text upon the Communion had, early in his life, made a profound impression upon him. Then the following words are quoted, concerning a text, namely"... that one who unworthily partakes of the sacrament *eateth and drinketh damnation to himself.*

I gather from this that the young Goethe feared participating in the sacrament of confession when he did not truly feel it. Like Jung, Goethe had a deeply religious nature, which he could only express *"extra ecclesiam."*[12] Raphael writes:

> Goethe's illness caused him acute physical as well as mental suffering...His mother...added to the personal care she gave her son the counseling of her most intimate friend, Fraulein Susannah Katharina von Klettenberg. She listened patiently to Goethe's intellectual quaverings and seekings, yet did not hesitate to tell him that his illness had occurred because he had not reconciled himself with God.[13]

It's worth noting that Fraulein von Klettenberg was a member of the Moravian Brethren, and had guided Goethe's mother and sister into that society. The Moravian Brethren were associated with heretical teachings going back to the Albigensians in the 13th century. A Dr. Metz, also a member of this circle, produced an alchemical cure for Goethe: Salt. Goethe recovered from his illness. He became fascinated with alchemy and began to study it.[14] In a footnote, Raphael quotes Jung in *Psychology and Alchemy*: "The *Rosarium philosophorum* says: Who therefore knows the salt and its solution knows the hidden secret of the wise men of old."[15] She refers to Paracelsus who made a correspondence between mercury (spirit), sulphur (soul) and salt (body).[16] We can surmise from

---

12  Jung, *Letters I*, p. 269.
13  Raphael, *Goethe and the Philosopher's Stone*, p. 10.
14  Raphael, *Goethe and the Philosopher's Stone*, p. 11.
15  Raphael, *Goethe and the Philosopher's Stone*, p. 23.
16  Raphael, *Goethe and the Philosopher's Stone*, p. 12.

this that Goethe, like his creature Faust, needed to descend out of his head into his body.

Goethe worked on *Faust* for more than 60 years from its conception around 1770, when he was a young man in his twenties, to its completion in 1831, a year before his death. The *Urfaust* (ca. 1772-75) probably included the Gretchen tragedy. Later fragments included the "Witch's Kitchen" and "Forest and Cave" scenes. At Schiller's repeated urging, he returned to Part I in 1797, but did not finish it until 1806. He began work on Part II in 1825.

Here is a part of a letter Goethe wrote to Wilhelm von Humboldt who urged Goethe to publish *Faust* during his lifetime. It is, Raphael tells us, his last letter, dated March 17$^{th}$, 1832. Goethe died a few days later.

> More than sixty years have passed since the conception of *Faust* was clear before me, in my youth…Of course it would give me infinite pleasure to dedicate and communicate, even in my lifetime, these very serious jests to my honored…and widely scattered friends, as well as to hear their answers. But the times are really so absurd and confused that I am convinced that my earnest, persevering endeavors about this curious construction would be ill rewarded, and, driven on the beach, they would lie like a wreck in ruins…[17]

Goethe felt that Part II would not be comprehensible, or acceptable in his times. So he never allowed it to be published. Even in our times it has run into difficulties. One of his 20$^{th}$ century translators, Walter Kaufman, doesn't bother to translate most of Part II, and scolds Goethe for having "indulged himself" and not striving for economy.[18] No wonder Goethe was nervous. I imagine him sealing up *Faust* Part II in a big package and sending it into the future to his great grandson, Jung.

Goethe swam easily in unconscious realms. David Luke, in his Introduction to the *Selected Verse*, describes the young Goethe: "He would frequently make poetry in a state approaching somnambulism or trance,

---

17  Raphael, *Goethe and the Philosopher's Stone*, p. 251.
18  Goethe, *Faust*, Edited by Walter Kaufman, p. 31.

sometimes waking and leaping out of bed in haste to scrawl down what had come to him before he forgot it, as he often did. The lines beginning 'Über allen Gipfeln...(1780), probably the most famous of all German lyrics, were suddenly scribbled on the wooden wall of a mountain hut.'"[19] This poem was woven into my childhood, often recited at bedtime by my German-speaking parents; it was an invocation to sleep.

> Über allen Gipfeln
> Ist Ruh
> In allen Wipfeln
> Spurest du
> Kaum enen Hauch
> Die Vögelein
> schweigen im Walde
> Warte nur, balde
> Ruhest du auch.

I like Milan Kundera's translation found in his novel *Immortality*,[20] in which Goethe is a character.

> On all hilltips
> There is peace,
> In all treetops
> You will hear
> Hardly a breath.
> Birds in the woods are silent.
> Just wait, soon
> You too will rest.

As you can hear, the poem is about sleep; it is about being part of the natural world, the hills, the trees, the birds; it is also about death.

---

19  Goethe, *Selected Verse*, Edited by David Luke, p. xxvi.
20  Kundera, *Immortality*, p. 26.

## Faust, The Storyline

> *Perhaps someday there will appear a poet courageous enough to give expression to the voices of the "mothers."*[21]

It is reckless to attempt to summarize the *Faust* story, since it is so complex, so rich and many faceted. But it is more reckless not to, since you need to have a feeling for the drama, to understand the myth. Like Job, Faust is set within the cosmic drama of a bet between God and the devil, about whether the devil can lead God's servant, in this case Faust, astray.

Faust is a famous professor and alchemist at the university. When we meet him he is in the grip of a midlife crisis. He's lost all joy in life and in learning. He tries to do a magical operation to invoke the Earth Spirit, hoping it will lead him to a larger life. But the Earth Spirit is much more powerful than Faust had imagined. Faust goes from inflation to deflation, and becomes suicidal. He says:

> I am not like a god! Too deeply now I feel
> This truth. I am a worm stuck in the dust…[22]

What saves Faust from drinking poison is the sound of Easter bells and the chorus singing "Christ is Risen!" Though he is no longer a practicing Christian, the familiar music reminds him of his childhood faith, and of life's possibilities.

Enter, Mephistopheles, in the form of a black poodle, who swells into a hippopotamus "with fearsome jaws and fiery eyes,"[23] and then steps out of a cloud into Faust's study in the form of a wandering scholar. Mephistopheles strikes a bargain with Faust: I'll be your slave in this life, if you'll be my slave in the next. Faust, who doesn't believe in the next life, has no problem with this.

Thus begins a series of adventures with Mephistopheles as Faust's constant companion. They leave the dry and dusty halls of academia for a tavern, then a witch's kitchen. With the help of Mephistopheles

---

21  Jung, *Letters II*, p. 387.
22  Goethe, *Faust*, Translated by David Luke, p. 23.
23  Goethe, *Faust*, p. 39.

and the witch, Faust becomes young again and falls in love with a naïve Christian girl, Gretchen, whom he seduces and impregnates. He has wild adventures at Walpurgis Night, a Witch's Sabbath. Part I ends with the Gretchen tragedy. Faust and she have inadvertently caused the death of her mother, her brother, and her child. Faust, who is ambivalent about how close he wants to be to her, tries, in the end, to save her. She is mad with grief, won't be saved. But when she dies, a voice from above proclaims that she is saved.

Part II. We are introduced to an empire in a state of decay. Mephistopheles helps the emperor by creating paper money, creating an inflationary situation. The emperor asks for more and more, insisting that Faust introduce him to the greatest lovers of all time—Paris and Helen. This requires Faust's descent to the realm of the Mothers, a very dangerous adventure. In a play within a play, we see Faust try to grab Helen from Paris. Big mistake! Mephistopheles saves him.

Meanwhile, back in Academia, Faust's former student Wagner is trying to create Homunculus, the little man who is the Philosopher's Stone, the goal of the alchemical opus. Homunculus does not come to life until Mephistopheles enters the scene. Homunculus becomes Faust's guardian angel and spirits him off to the pagan South. Here, with Mephistopheles' help, Faust wins Helen. In fact, Faust gets pretty much everything his greedy ego demands, becoming a great robber baron and land developer. In the end, he causes the death of two good old souls, Philemon and Baucis.

The fate of Faust's soul is controversial, for Gretchen (shades of Dante's Beatrice), intervenes and brings his soul to heaven. Has he gotten away with murder? Or is this a moment of grace? By giving himself so fully to life, by living his shadow, has he become, in his death, whole?

## Faust as Jung's Myth

*The inner voice is a "Lucifer..."*[24]

---

24 Jung, "The Development of the Personality," *CW* 17, ¶ 319.

The themes in *Faust* dramatize Jung's central psychological concepts. The devil, Mephistopheles, is Faust's shadow. And though this devil is a trickster, of questionable morality, he brings life and pleasure back into Faust's dried up life. As Joseph Henderson wrote:

> In accepting the wager of Mephistopheles, Faust put himself in the power of a "shadow" figure. Faust had failed to live out to the full an important part of his early life. He was accordingly, an unreal or incomplete person who lost himself in a fruitless quest for metaphysical goals that failed to materialize.[25]

When Jung, at his mother's urging, read *Faust*, he writes:

> It poured into my soul like a miraculous balm. "Here at last," I thought, "is someone who takes the devil seriously and even concludes a blood pact with him—with the adversary who had the power to frustrate God's plan to make a perfect world…"

> Faust was plainly a bit of a windbag. I had the impression that the weight of the drama and its significance lay chiefly on the side of Mephistopheles…whose whole figure made the deepest impression on me…Mephistopheles and the great initiation at the end remained for me a wonderful and mysterious experience on the fringes of my conscious world…

> At last I had found confirmation that there were or had been people who saw evil and its universal power, and—more important—the mysterious role it played in delivering man from darkness and suffering. To that extent Goethe became, in my eyes, a prophet.[26]

Who is this Mephistopheles who made such a deep impression on the young Jung? Mephistopheles refers to his "old crony, the serpent,"[27]

---

25 Henderson, "Ancient Myths and Modern Man," *Man and His Symbols*, p. 121.
26 Jung, *MDR*, p. 60.
27 Goethe, *Faust*, translated by Barker Fairley, p. 30.

and in *Aion*, Jung refers to "Mephistopheles, whose "aunt is the snake"[28] (as) Goethe's version of the alchemical familiar Mercurius." Jung says of the snake that it "signifies evil and darkness on the one hand and wisdom on the other. Its unrelatedness, coldness and dangerousness express the instinctuality that, with ruthless cruelty, rides roughshod over all moral and any other human wishes."[29] That's a good description of Mephistopheles. He is both a seducer and initiator into larger consciousness, like the snake in the Garden of Eden; but he is cruel and inhuman, as in the Gretchen tragedy when Faust is beginning to show some real feeling for her plight.

> Faust: In misery! In despair. Pitiably wandering about the country for so long, and now a prisoner...In utter ruin... And meanwhile you lull me with vulgar diversions...
>
> Mephistopheles: She is not the first.[30]

There is a wisdom inherent in what Jung calls "the natural mind [that] says the terrible things, the absolutely straight and ruthless things."[31] This shows up just a few lines later when Mephistopheles challenges Faust to take responsibility for his own behavior:

> Who was it that brought her to ruin? Was it me or was it you?[32]

In Edinger's invaluable book, *Goethe's Faust: Notes for a Jungian Commentary*, he writes of Mephistopheles:

> He is the spirit of negation, Carlyle's "Everlasting No," and the principle of heroic defiance exemplified by Milton's Lucifer. He is the power principle on which the very existence of the ego is based. To say no is the primal act of *separatio*, the act

---

28 Jung, "The Structure and Dynamics of the Self," in *Aion*, *CW* 9 ii, ¶ 371.
29 Jung, *CW* 9 ii, p. 234.
30 Goethe, *Faust*, translated by Luke, p. 1.
31 Edinger, *Goethe's Faust*, p. 32.
32 Goethe, *Faust*, translated by Fairley, p. 77.

> which establishes the ego as the arbiter of its own existence. It is the original sin that generates initial consciousness.³³

> What does it mean to make a pact with the Devil? From the standpoint of conventional consciousness it means having commerce with evil, the forbidden thing, the irrational, the repressed, the denied, the despicable—in a word, with the unconscious…

> The theme of service, who is to serve whom, is highly relevant. It points to the ultimate fact of individuation, namely, the fact that the ego is fated to serve the Self.³⁴

And Jung writes:

> Mephistopheles is far more than sexuality—he is also power; in fact, he is practically the whole life of Faust, barring that part which is taken up with thinking and research.³⁵

In an early essay, "The Type Problem in Poetry," Jung describes Faust as a "medieval Prometheus" who defies the "accepted gods."³⁶ In that passage, he quotes Mephistopheles' self-description, a phrase we find quoted over and over again in Jung's work: "part of that force which always tries to do evil and always does good." That, in a nutshell, describes the ethical dilemma of the shadow.

Mephistopheles' realm is much larger than the Christian worldview. He cavorts with witches, has a snake as a crony, transforms himself into a dog, a hippopotamus, an elephant, and then into human form, performs all kinds of magic, is, Jung tells us, "the strange son of chaos,"³⁷ In his presence, things come to life—Faust, Homunculus. He is "part… of the darkness that gave birth to light. Light that in its arrogance challenges Mother night."³⁸ Jung quotes this famous phrase in *Mysterium*, in

---

33   Edinger, *Goethe's Faust*, pp. 29-30.
34   Edinger, *Goethe's Faust*, p. 32.
35   Jung, "The Type Problem in Poetry," *CW* 6, ¶ 345.
36   Jung, "The Type Problem in Poetry," *CW* 6, ¶¶ 315-316.
37   Jung, "Gnostic Symbols of the Self," *CW* 6, ¶ 325.
38   Jung, "Gnostic Symbols of the Self," *CW* 6, ¶, 21.

his description of Luna, who he writes, "is really the mother of the sun, which means, psychologically, that the unconscious is pregnant with consciousness and gives birth to it. It is the night, which is older than the day."[39]

In Goethe, Jung tells us[40] "the *worship of the soul* [is] symbolized by the *worship* of woman." Gretchen, Edinger explains, represents "the first stage in the development of the anima, the instinctual stage."[41] Her death represents a failed coniunctio. But Mephistopheles, in his chaotic way, leads Faust onward. We find ourselves in an empire in total disarray. Mephistopheles has taken the role of the Emperor's fool. Here is how the situation is described by members of the State Council:

> Lawlessness becomes law and has its way, and a whole world of wrong is the result…The whole world is breaking up and destroying all decency and propriety…
>
> Everything's on borrowed money, the beds we sleep in and the bread we eat.[42]

Sound familiar? It could be a description of the economic bubble that burst in 2008, ushering in the Great Recession. Mephistopheles, like the con men of our own time, comes up with a scheme involving paper money, based on the "futures" of mining treasure from the earth. The empire looks rich now, though we know it's a trick, and the Emperor puts Mephistopheles and Faust in charge of the underground. On top of all this, the Emperor says, he wants to "see Paris and Helen right away."[43] This, we learn, is no mean feat.

---

39  Jung, "The Personification of the Opposites," *CW* 14, ¶ 219.
40  Jung, "The Type Problem in Poetry," *CW* 6, ¶ 375.
41  Edinger, *Goethe's Faust*, pp. 44-45.
42  Goethe, *Faust*, Translated by Barker Fairley, pp. 85-86.
43  Goethe, *Faust*, Translated by Fairley, p. 105.

## Descent to the Mothers

> *The creative process has a feminine quality, and the creative work arises from unconscious depths—we might truly say from the realm of the Mothers.*[44]

Goethe describes Faust's descent to the Mothers in an amazing passage, one that I believe describes the essence of mystical as well as creative experience: the courage required to venture into the unknown, into the forbidden, into nothingness. If you are lucky you will have a key.

Mephistopheles: There are goddesses throned in solitude, outside of place, outside of time. It makes me uneasy even to talk about them. They are the Mothers.

Faust: (*startled*) The Mothers.

Mephistopheles: Does it give you the shivers?

Faust: The Mothers. The Mothers. It sounds so queer.

Mephistopheles: Queer it is. Goddesses unknown to mortal men, hardly to be named by them. You'll need to dig deep to reach them…

Faust: Show me the way.

Mephistopheles: There is no way. You'll enter the untrodden, the untreadable, the unpermitted, the impermissible. Are you ready? There'll be no locks or bolts. You'll be pushed about from one emptiness to another. Have you any notion what emptiness is? Barrenness?…You won't hear the tread of your own feet. You'll find nowhere to rest your head.

Faust: You talk like the biggest mystagogue that ever fooled his simple pupil. Only you're in reverse. You're sending me into nothingness, where I'm supposed to improve myself in my art…In this nothing of yours I hope to find the everything.

Mephistopheles: I see you understand the devil and I'll give you a word of approval before you go. Here. Take this key.

Faust: That little thing.

---

44  Jung, "Psychology and Literature," *CW* 15, ¶ 159.

Mephistopheles: Take hold of it and don't underrate it.

Faust: It's growing in my hand, it's shining, flashing.

Mephistopheles:...This key will nose out the way for you! Follow its lead. It'll conduct you to the Mothers...When you come to a glowing tripod you'll know you're as far down as you can go. By the light it throws you'll see the Mothers. Some sitting, some standing or walking about. It just depends. Formation, transformation, the eternal mind eternally communing with itself, surrounded by the forms of all creation. They won't see you. They only see ghosts. You'll be in great danger and you'll need a stout heart. Go straight up to the tripod and touch it with your key.[45]

In *Symbols of Transformation*, his early work, before his break from Freud, Jung responds to this passage with a commentary on the symbolism of the key. I read it as a description of how his creative libido was leading him out of Freud's too narrow framework, into the wild chaotic world of his great grandfather Goethe, and the collective unconscious.

> [The key] is the libido, which is not only creative and procreative, but possesses an intuitive faculty, a strange power to "smell the right place," almost as if it were a live creature with an independent life of its own...
>
> It is purposive, like sexuality itself...The "realm of the Mothers" has not a few connections with the womb, with the matrix, which frequently symbolizes the creative aspect of the unconscious. This libido is a force of nature, good and bad at once, or morally neutral. Uniting himself with it, Faust succeeds in accomplishing his real life's work...In the realm of the Mothers he finds the tripod, the Hermetic vessel in which the "royal marriage" is consummated. But he needs the phallic wand in order to bring off the greatest wonder of all—the creation of Paris and Helen [the coniunctio]. The insignificant-looking tool in Faust's hand is the dark creative power of the unconscious, which reveals itself to those who follow its dictates and is indeed capable of working miracles.[46]

---

45  Goethe, *Faust*, Translated by Barker Fairley, pp. 106-108.
46  Jung, "Introduction," *CW* 5, ¶ 182.

Back in *Faust* Part II we are watching a play within a play—we see Faust, watching Paris and Helen. Faust is transported by Helen's beauty.

Faust: Do I see with my eyes? Or is it deep in my inner mind that the source of beauty is thus poured out before me? My fearful journey has brought a marvelous reward. How futile the world was, before it was opened to me…The fair form that once delighted me…was mere froth beside this. To you I owe the springs of every action and the quintessence of passion.[47]

Faust has encountered his anima. Overcome with passion, Faust grabs Helen away from Paris, violating time's boundaries, myth's boundaries, plunging from realm to realm. *Explosion*. Mephistopheles throws him over his shoulder.

Back in Academia, Faust is unconscious. It takes major interventions by Mephistopheles and Homunculus, the loveable little creature who keeps trying to get born, to bring Faust and Helen back together again. This time, Faust woos her with respect and attentiveness, and their coniunctio produces the child, Euphorion. But Euphorion is not long for this world. Like Icarus, he flies too high and dies. Helen, unwilling to leave him alone in the underworld, follows him. Faust, at Mephistopheles prompting, grabs her veil.

Jung comments on Faust's action in grabbing Helen in *Psychology and Alchemy*:

> By identifying with Paris, Faust brings the coniunctio back from its projected state into the sphere of personal psychological experience and thus into consciousness. This crucial step means nothing less than the solution of the alchemical riddle, and at the same time the redemption of a previously unconscious part of the personality. But every increase in consciousness harbours the danger of inflation, as is shown very clearly in Faust's superhuman powers.[48]

Though we have seen real psychological development in Faust, as he is able to woo and win Helen, his inflation and mad power drive turn

---

47  Goethe, *Faust*, Translated by Barker Fairley, pp. 112-113.
48  Jung, "Epilogue," *CW* 12, ¶ 559.

him into a robber baron and land developer. When we meet him toward the end of the play and toward the end of his life, he is busy controlling the deep blue sea, stealing its territory for housing developments. He wants all the land he can see, including the small cottage belonging to Baucis and Philemon. He gives Mephistopheles the task of clearing the old couple out. By accident, they are killed in a fire. Jung tells it this way in *Psychology and Alchemy*:

> In his blind urge for superhuman power, Faust brought about the murder of Philemon and Baucis. Who are these two humble old people? When the world had become godless and no longer offered a hospitable retreat to the divine strangers Jupiter and Mercury, it was Philemon and Baucis who received the superhuman guests.[49]

You'd think, with so much sin on Faust's soul, that Mephistopheles' long servitude would be rewarded at Faust's death. But something very mysterious happens at the end of Goethe's *Faust*—as Faust is dying, Mephistopheles, the ultimate trickster gets tricked by a chorus of pretty boy angels. He, the magician and enchanter, finds himself enchanted.

> I like the look of them, these darling boys…So lovely, so kissable…You're so enticing, you're getting prettier all the time.[50]

And while he ogles them and suffers pangs of desire and love, thus becoming more human, those boy angels make off with Faust's immortal part. Faust is transformed into Doctor Marianus, whom Jung tells us was "one of the most spiritual of all alchemists."[51] The spirit of Gretchen welcomes him to the heights of eternity; he is blessed by the feminine in all her forms, including the spirit of the prostitute, Mary of Egypt and the *Mater Gloriosa*, the mother of us all.

Jung writes:

> Faust's redemption began at his death. The divine, Promethean character he has preserved all his life fell away from him

---

49  Jung, "Epilogue," *CW* 12, ¶ 561.
50  Goethe, *Faust*, Translated by Barker Fairley, p. 199.
51  Jung, "The Symbolic Life," *CW* 18, ¶ 1699.

only at death, with his rebirth. Psychologically, this means that the Faustian attitude must be abandoned before the individual can become an integrated whole.[52]

The *numinosum* that greets Faust's "immortal part" in heaven was foreshadowed by the earlier symbol of the coniunctio, the "divine images of Paris and Helen [as they] float up from the tripod of the Mothers."[53] Jung continues:

> The symbol [of the coniunctio] is a pointer to the onward course of life, beckoning the libido toward a still distant goal—but a goal that henceforth will burn unquenchably within him, so that his life, kindled as by a flame, moves steadily towards the far-off beacon.[54]

Edinger tells us that, "*Mysterium Coniunctionis* can…be considered an exhaustive commentary on Goethe's *Faust*…"[55] Goethe's *Faust* burnt in Jung like a flame—guide and companion through all his long opus; it was his myth.

Faust ends with these famous words, spoke by the Chorus Mysticus:

> Alles Vergangliche
>
> Ist nur ein Gleichnis;
>
> Das Unzulängliche
>
> Hier wirds Ereignis;
>
> Das Unbeschreibliche
>
> Hier ist es getan
>
> Das Ewig-Weibliche
>
> Zieht uns hinan.[56]

This mysterious and haunting final passage is, as the critic Hans Eichner observes, "quite untranslatable."[57] I like Edinger's rendition the best:

---

52  Jung, *CW* 6, ¶ 317.
53  Jung, *CW* 6, ¶ 202.
54  Jung, *CW* 6, ¶ 202.
55  Edinger, *Goethe's Faust*, p. 67.
56  *Faust: A Norton Critical Edition*, translated by Walter Arndt, p. 616.
57  *Faust: A Norton Critical Edition*, translated by Walter Arndt, p. 616.

> All things transitory
> Are only symbols;
> The insufficient
> Here finds fulfillment
> The indescribable
> Here it is done
> The Eternal Womanly
> Draws us above.[58]

To me this ending is an invocation of the mystery of transformation. Goethe's great drama brings the inaccessible into being, performs the indescribable, and lifts us into the realm of the "eternal feminine."

## Our Myth

> *Goethe became, in my eyes, a prophet.*[59]

If Goethe is a prophet of our time, what is it he prophesied? Edinger gives us a way of orienting ourselves in the great flow of the cultural unconscious when he writes:

> In the sixteenth century the God-image fell out of heaven… and landed in the human psyche. In the course of this transition from heaven to earth it undergoes an enantiodromia from Christ to Antichrist. This event paves the way for Faust's encounter with Mephistopheles.[60]

Edinger is referring here to the Faust legend, of which there are many versions. It all began with a historical person, a Dr. John Faustus, who lived from 1480 to 1540.[61] Dr. Faustus was said to be a sorcerer, a black magician, an astrologer, a shyster, a seducer of young boys. A chapbook published some fifty years after his death, called, "*Historia von D. Johann Faustus, the notorious Sorcerer and Nigromancer*" achieved instantaneous

---

58 Edinger, *Goethe's Faust*, p. 89.
59 Jung, *MDR*, p. 60.
60 Edinger, *Goethe's Faust*, p. 14.
61 Edinger, *Goethe's Faust*, p. 13.

popular success. The chapbook contains references to Faust's deal with the devil, his journey to hell, and his conjuring up of Helen of Troy.[62]

Edinger points out that Dr. Faustus' life was roughly contemporary to the Renaissance, the Reformation, the Scientific Revolution, and to the lives of Leonardo, Columbus, Machiavelli, Erasmus, Copernicus, Luther, and Paracelsus. The early Faust legend is about a thoroughly despicable character who gets his just punishment. Goethe's *Faust*, as we have seen, is much more complicated. He snaps his "fingers at heaven and hell"[63] isn't concerned about traditional notions of good and evil, thinks maybe he's a god. He's rather like us.

When the God-image fell into the human psyche, we began to confuse ourselves with the gods; we wanted to control the natural world and the deep blue sea; we wanted to penetrate all the mysteries. Goethe's *Faust* is a prophesy of our collective hubris, our restless desire to explore all the worlds and to feed our hungry egos. It is a prophesy of our ethical dilemma.

We want to touch the moon and bring back moon dust. We zoom around Mars and connive to scoop up its ice, its gases, for our investigation. What used to be the subject of myth and of poetry, Luna and Mars, is now the object of rockets and scientific study. As we know from Goethe and from Jung, there is something marvelous about all this exploration, something that widens consciousness, frees us from the old gods. We know this also from the powerful experience of the astronauts who first landed on the moon—they saw our planet's fragile beauty. That image of a delicate blue globe in a dark sky pervades our collective consciousness.

But we also know from Goethe and Jung the terrible danger of inflation, of hubris, in the accumulation of such power and knowledge. Theodore Ziolkowski, a professor of German and Comparative Literature at Princeton, argues that the myths of Adam, Prometheus, and Faust have in common what he calls, "The Sin of Knowledge," which is how he names his book. He writes:

---

62 Ziolkowski, *The Sin of Knowledge*, pp. 52, 58.
63 Goethe, *Faust*, Translated by Barker Fairley, p. 8.

"Faustian," thanks to Oswald Spengler, designates not simply an individual who makes a compromise with evil forces in order to achieve his ends, but also an entire technological age that applies intellect often destructively to the subordination of nature.[64]

Ziolkowski quotes the *Confessions* of Augustine as referring to, "a form of temptation that is even more dangerous than the temptations of the flesh: the desire for experience and knowledge…that he calls *curiositas*,[65] In our time, we highly value *curiositas*, but pay dearly for it.

One of the ways we've understood the myth of Faust in our lifetimes has been in connection with the Atom bomb. Ziolkowski refers to the frequency with which the physicist, "Oppenheimer was portrayed as the Faustian figure who made a bargain with the devil"[66] in order to create the first Atomic bomb. This theme was background to John Adams' powerful opera, *Dr. Atomic*.

But it is not just Oppenheimer who is Faust. We are all Faust. We have made a bargain with the devil for enormous power over the earth. We have committed crimes against nature and humanity for the sake of more land, more energy, more destructive capacity. We have taken too much out of the sea and put into it toxic waste: mercury, PCPs, oil spills. These come back in the fish we eat to poison us. We are Faust in our lust for speed and power, for bigger houses, bigger cars, more wealth—in our greed, our insatiable appetite for material goods. We want to understand everything, to split the atom, to change the DNA of seeds and of animals. We are addicted to growth, to the crazy idea that our economy is only healthy if it keeps getting bigger and bigger.

We have lost our connection to the sacred, the numinous, the mysteries. We have lost awe and gratitude for the Spirit of the Earth. We are soiling our nest. The Earth Spirit responds with earthquakes, hurricanes, tornadoes, fires, floods, cyclones, tsunamis—every way she can slap us about, wake us up, remind us we are not gods, but small creatures entirely dependent on her. The earth is not our servant, not our

---

64 Ziolkowski, *Sin of Knowledge*, p. 45.
65 Ziolkowski, *Sin of Knowledge*, p. 56.
66 Ziolkowski, *Sin of Knowledge*, p. 150.

resource—she is our only home. We have murdered that humble old couple Baucis and Philemon, we have killed off their connection to the divine. Our Faustian guilt is about rising sea levels, the fate of the polar bear, the fate of the salmon, the fate of the honeybee.

Like Jung, we need to create a shrine to Philemon and Baucis, a way to atone for our guilt. The bad news is that we're getting painfully conscious of the damage we've done. The good news is that we're getting painfully conscious of the damage we've done. Faust needs to be transformed in us, to get curious about sustainability and how to preserve species; we need to find a humbler way of life.

The whole cornucopia of life is in *Faust*: love, war, carnival, empire, academia, the Church, the Witches Sabbath. As Heine says "*Faust*...is really as spacious as the Bible, and like it, embraces heaven and earth, together with man and his exegesis."[67] I find much solace in its wild chaotic life, the promiscuity of its imagery which breaks categories, mixes up myths from various cultures and times, gives voice to everyone: the Furies, the Fates, the Graces, gnomes, satyrs, witches, an Olive Branch with Fruits, a Wreath of Golden Ripe corn. It is the *anima mundi*. In the outermost frame story, before we get to the Lord, his angels, and the devil making their bet about Faust, the director, the poet and the clown, argue about how best to put on the show. The poet longs to be young again. The clown believes that "old age brings out the true child in us all." The director wants to get the show on the road. He's concerned with scenery. He wants lots of it:

> You have sun and moon at your disposal and stars in plenty. Water, fire, rocks, beasts, birds…So on this little stage of ours we can run through the whole of creation, and with fair speed make your say from heaven through the world to hell.[68]

All this dramatic capacity, all this chaos and wild fertility of the imagination, is ours too, if we can experience the world we live in as alive. And yet, the play hinges on a single simple moment. As they bargain for Faust's soul in Part I, Faust says:

---

67 *Faust: A Norton Critical Edition*, translated by Walter Arndt, p. 442.
68 Goethe, *Faust*, Translated by Barker Fairley, p. 5.

> If ever the passing moment is such that I wish it not to pass, and I say to it, "You are beautiful, stay awhile," then let that be the finish. The clock can stop. You can put me in chains and ring the death-bell.[69]

At the end of his life, Faust is approached by Care, who wonders if he has ever experienced her before.[70] Faust has a rare moment of self-reflection: "I've just raced through the world, seizing what I fancied by the hair of its head...I've simply desired and fulfilled my desire and desired again."[71]

Care, disrespected by Faust, blinds him. But in the dark, his "inner light shines clear." And that is when he says to the passing moment: "Bleib einmal, du bit so schön." Stay awhile, you are so beautiful. This moment is what the great religions teach: satori, enlightenment, grace. It is the moment of epiphany of which the poet writes. It comes in contrast to the great confusion and profusion of life that Faust has known, and it foreshadows his salvation by the grace of the eternal feminine. Moments like this when we hold the world sacred, when things slow down and are filled with light, touch our souls with the numinous. But we also crave the wild ride of indulging our senses, exploring the fertility of life and the imagination. This pair of opposites is hard to hold, but we need them both to make it through our Faustian dilemmas. For the solution, as Jung says, is religious.

One day I was in my car, about to drive across the bridge to meet my husband Dan for dinner in San Francisco, when I heard on the news that the bridge was closed. A man was threatening suicide. In the mysterious ways that poems happen, this experience began a poem, "Faust on the Bridge." I knew nothing about this man except that he was driving a red BMW, and that he was suicidal, but he became Everyman, or Every Faust, to me. Here is the poem:

---

69  *Faust*, Translated by Barker Fairley, p. 25.
70  *Faust*, Translated by Barker Fairley, p. 194.
71  *Faust*, Translated by Barker Fairley, p. 195.

## faust on the bridge

> *Bleib einmal, du bist so schön!*
> *(Stay a moment, you are so beautiful!)*
> —Goethe's Faust

don't know your name   don't know your story   just know
you got out of your red BMW on the western side of Treasure
Island  leapt to the edge of the bridge
                    and threatened to jump

there are those who are angry   those who wish you'd just
get it over with   but I who was planning to drive
that very bridge whose traffic you've snarled up for hours
I who was forced to abandon my car   take Bart   can see   thanks to you
this sudden glimpse of loveliness   before the train
descends into the dark   and I  say to you who are so certain
you can't take another moment of whatever your agony is
you who've slashed your face with a razor   who stand there bleeding:

*stay a moment   uncover your face   look!*
*the bay is a glittering opal   in a setting of gray blue hills*
*there are towers   pyramids   a shining city   even Faust*
*who wanted everything   traded in his poison cup for such*
*a moment   I ask you   when you were a child   was there a lake?*
*did pieces of light dance on the water? was there a tree you'd climb*
*up to the  perfect branch that let the wind sway you?   let it sway*

*you again   let the holy light on the water*
*enter the ache in your heart   a whole city has slowed down*
*around you   brother cannot get across the bridge*
*to meet brother   lovers are late for their dates   I climb stone steps*
*out of the underground   to meet my Dan at a small cafe   white blossoms*
*toss in the breeze   gold gleams in our chardonnay   we speak*
                                                    *of you*[72]

---

72  Lowinsky, first published in *The Litchfield Review*.

# SECTION THREE

# WHAT IS AFRICA TO ME?

## Chapter 5

## My Home is Over Jordan[1]

*my people are the people of the pianoforte and the violin*
*Mozart people    Bach people    Hallelujah people...*

*your people are the drum beat people    the field holler people*
*the conjure people    blues people    jubilee people    people who*
*talk straight to God*[2]

### Deep River

*My people found in the grandeur of the Biblical word and poetry a fountain of...solace. From out the horizon of their tragic lot rose a sublime illumination...that drew inspiration in...the revelations of the Bible... Words and music became one... religious ecstasy as well as sheer intoxication with the sound of the Word...*[3]

There are borderlands which only music and poetry can evoke; here, our cultural stories begin. They hover between myth and memory, between

---

1  Lowinsky, published in an earlier version in *Psychological Perspectives*, Vol. 52, Issue 2/2009.
2  Lowinsky, from the poem, "Your People are My People," first published in *New Millennium Writings*.
3  Roland Hayes, *My Favorite Spirituals*, p. 13.

the realm of the ancestors and our "home over Jordan," between the Christian testament and the African oracle, between the Jewish and the African diasporas, in the haunted realms between black folk and white folk. In these stories we were slaves, taken from our native land by force. We were forced from the land of our ancestors, where we knew every tree, every stone. We walked the trail of tears. Many died. We escaped our homeland with just the clothes on our backs, persecuted for our religion, our politics, our class.

Sometimes another story comes along, one that changes how we see our origins, that shakes loose the old convictions, opens the door to a new myth. This happened to me once when I visited the ghost of Black Mountain College in a beautiful valley in the foothills of North Carolina. Black Mountain was a radical school, famous for being an experimental community and for counting among its faculty and students some of the great talents of mid and late 20$^{th}$ century America including John Cage, Merce Cunningham, Jacob Lawrence, Ruth Asawa, Charles Olson, Robert Creeley and Robert Duncan. The school opened in 1933, and closed its doors, for lack of money, in 1956.

My parents, refugee Jews from Germany, were on the faculty of Black Mountain in the 1940s. My father was a musicologist and a pianist, my mother a violinist and violist. I spent the first years of my life there. I heard stories of Black Mountain all my life, that it was exciting, crazy, politically intense and difficult. My father took pride in being on the committee that desegregated Black Mountain, making it the first white southern college to accept blacks. He took pride in having invited Roland Hayes and Carol Brice, African American singers of the classical repertoire, to perform at Black Mountain.

I had always seen myself as a child of catastrophe, of war, of the annihilation of my people in Europe. What I hadn't remembered was the beauty of my first landscape. A lyrical campus by Lake Eden, in sight of two swelling hills, which, I was told, the students called "Mae West." In a borderland between memory and imagination, I could see my little towheaded baby self toddling on these paths, friend to the willows and the maples, enchanted by birdsong and the great goddess Mae West. The essence of everything I am and love was right there, by Lake Eden, in view of the female shape of the hills and their reflection in water, that and the intensity of intellectual and artistic life that flowed around me. I was filled with longing: I needed to hear Roland Hayes sing.

Roland Hayes' voice is hard to find nowadays. He was as well-known in his day as were Paul Robeson and Marian Anderson, both of whom he mentored. He was a pioneer in the borderlands between African-American and European-American cultures. He introduced the beauty and power of spirituals to concert audiences in Europe and America. Sadly, he's been forgotten. A search online came up with a CD containing a strange combination: the actor Charlton Heston reading from the Gospels, and Roland Hayes singing spirituals. Listening to Hayes' beautiful tenor voice filled me with a peculiar mix of longing, grief, and a deep sense of homecoming.

After that journey to North Carolina, I asked my mother to reminisce about Roland Hayes, whom she first met at Black Mountain College in 1945. Listening to her tell the story of the concert at which Brice and Hayes sang, the obvious struck me. All this had happened when I was two years old, a toddler of German Jewish origin in North Carolina. It was the summer of 1945. That was the summer the war ended. That was the summer the United States dropped atomic bombs on Hiroshima and Nagasaki. That was the summer my father organized a desegregated concert in the segregated south. My father, my mother told me, prompted the student ushers to be polite but firm. People should sit wherever they wanted. "We were afraid that the Ku Klux Klan would burn the college down," she told me. That did not happen. An integrated audience of over 300 people heard Brice and Hayes sing. The concert was a great success. Julia Feininger, wife of the painter Lionel Feininger, spoke of Hayes' performance:

> His concert…was beautiful beyond words…It is not the voice alone; it is the whole man, the musician, the artist… the rhythm, well it is very difficult to describe it in words, as it is sound and picture in one and the fourthpouring soul of the man. And the astonishing thing is, that he sings Bach

and negro spirituals...with equal fervor and religious feeling, understanding, deep conviction.)[4]

A two-year-old would understand none of this. But she would feel the tension, the passion, the elation when all went well. Did she hear the concert? Did Roland Hayes come back to the cottage where she lived? Did she hear him sing spirituals? Those songs still flow in her soul like a deep river; they have sustained her in unseen ways all her days. In her child's mythology, "Let My People Go" was about black slaves in America as well as Jewish slaves in Egypt; so was the story her people told at Passover. Her father encouraged this, making spirituals a part of the family Sabbath ritual. The chariot swung down to carry her to sleep at night.

Why did those songs mean so much to me? Was it that they described the world I saw, full of myth and mystery, a world in which chariots swing low to carry a suffering soul home? Did they bring the bible stories my father told me to life in song? Did they assure me that the unbearable can be borne if one can sing about it, if one can get carried away on the wings of the imagination? Did they teach me that myth is alive; that a simple mythic refrain, "Go Down Moses," can transform feeling and merge traditions, that song used as prayer, as exhortation, is transformative?

History swirls about us, collective and personal. There I was, so young a child, my imagination forming amidst all that music and conversation, all that natural beauty, all that symbol making and arguing, all that political intensity, all that passion for the arts. How strange that so many of my influences would pass through this place. Charles Olson would invite Jung to the college. Jung was ill, but sent Marie-Louise von Franz in his stead. She gave a series of lectures on folklore, mythology and hermetic philosophy. This was in 1953; my family was long gone.

Poets would come in those years after we were gone, who would be major influences on my work. I never crossed paths in person with Robert Creeley or Robert Duncan. But they came to me in books when I was a young woman. When I heard them referred to as Black Mountain Poets, I knew they were kin. It is as though Black Mountain, that funny

---

4  Mary Emma Harris, *The Arts at Black Mountain*, pp. 101, 104.

little borderland of the universe, was an alchemical vessel in which the stuff of my life was cooking, long before I had words to describe it.

What a gift to be born into all of this. There must have been fairies at my cradle. They gave me the gifts of the mountains, the willows, green lawns, the lake, the gift of spending my baby years amidst all that music and art-making, among people who understood that the arts were central, as my father's colleague Heinrich Jalowitz put it, in "the stupendous task of reconstructing our shaken world."[5]

It is strange to be able to read about the world of one's childhood, the world one's parents moved in, the drama that shaped their young psyches. Mary Emma Harris published her beautiful book, *The Arts at Black Mountain*, full of art, photographs and history, in the late 80s. My parents show up often, most notably in a lovely photograph of a musical performance, my father at the piano, my mother in a stunning evening gown, playing the violin. The historian Martin Duberman interviewed hundreds of people, including my parents, in the late 60s, to research his book: *Black Mountain: An Exploration in Community*. Reading his book is like peering through a window at my young father, embroiled in the controversies of Black Mountain in the 40s.

My father's been dead a generation, but I'm still trying to figure him out. Was he all bluster and brag? He always told stories of himself that made him the hero, like the one about being on the committee that desegregated Black Mountain. But wait, here in the intricate political maneuverings detailed in Duberman's retelling, my father is on the conservative side in the schism of 1944. He votes against the admission of blacks, though he compromises on one black student for a summer program. Eric Bentley, who was to become a renowned Brecht scholar, was the rebel angel of the radical faction. He called my father an "old maid."[6]

Hey Dad—did you really lead your southern college into integration?

The past flutters in the breeze like a prayer flag, like lovely see-through curtains with designs from another time. I can't pin it down; there is no certainty, no substance. What I would give to be able to push aside those

---

5   Harris, *The Arts at Black Mountain*, p. 94.
6   Martin Duberman, *Black Mountain: An Exploration in Community*, p. 196.

curtains and know what that baby heard, smelled, saw, dreamt. What I would give to be able to talk to the people whose faces and voices were part of my earliest impressions, to ask them, with what I know now of life, how it was then. The next best thing is reading Duberman. Hundreds of interviews done 30 years ago by those then still alive, each with their own axe to grind. These were people with hard edges. Many had been shaped by horror and loss. In Duberman's nuanced and balanced narration, I catch some of the subtleties. My father's stance had more to do with his recent experience in Europe. He was one of a group of new faculty, German Jewish refugees, many of them middle aged and very distinguished. My father was younger, in his late 30s, but he had written a famous dissertation and was known in his field. The Europeans were offended by the brash provocations of the Bentley faction, its youth and inexperienced idealism. They'd had painful experiences with the German communists, whose machinations helped bring Hitler to power. They didn't trust radical political positions. And they felt disrespected by Bentley.

What blasted the place open and caused the schism was not racial but sexual. Two young women students took off hitchhiking to visit their beloved professor Bentley, who was teaching at Fisk for the summer. They were arrested for "loitering," a euphemism for prostitution. Why had no one stopped them? They had spoken of their plans to at least one faculty member. A huge fight ensued about faculty attitudes toward students. Were they to be supported and listened to, or was that coddling? Should they be confronted? Or should they be left alone to suffer and find their own resources? I knew these fights from later childhood when they happened between my parents.

This schism resulted in several faculty leaving. In the aftermath, my father worked hard to shift the painful feelings in the community. It was indeed he who led the effort to integrate Black Mountain. Duberman writes:

> With Lowinsky, rather than Bentley…advocating further strides on integration, neither subversion of the college nor the creation of a communist cell could be charged as ulterior motives. Lowinsky was judiciousness itself; neither his poli-

tics nor his private life could be thought in any way to compromise the "purity of his motives." He proceeded, moreover, with a pacing...exquisitely balanced between caution and tenacity...

Not only did Lowinsky locate "[black] students for the summer institutes, but he also managed to persuade two outstanding black artists, Carol Brice (at the beginning of her career and not yet famous) and Roland Hayes (at the end of his career, and world famous) to join the institute as guest faculty members...

Roland Hayes...had never heard Carol Brice sing and was so taken with her, that afterward, at a party at the Lowinskys, he sang for her his own unpublished arrangements of Negro spirituals and promised her copies for use at her concerts. Hayes and his family stayed for two weeks and had an enormous impact on the community. He was a magical storyteller and a charming man, and talked for hours on end about his personal experiences...and his lifelong work with black music. [7]

So Roland Hayes did come to my family's cottage! He sang the Aframerican (his term) spirituals he had collected and arranged. I was a baby in that cottage. Was I asleep when Hayes sang? Or was I in one of my parents' arms, or being handed from person to person in the crowded room? What does a dreamy child take in of the world around her? Of its passions, its sorrows, its schisms, its good works? If such a baby is born during the worst of times for her people, to a father whose mother has just died in a concentration camp, and whose father is on his way to Auschwitz on a train, soon to be bombed by the Allies, if her parents are suddenly in a position to do something about terrible racial injustice, if they give concerts at black high schools and colleges in the South, in order to attract black faculty and students, wouldn't there be a shift in the cosmos of her baby self, some opening to the possibility of goodness and life? If she heard Roland Hayes sing "Deep River," about the home

---

7 Duberman, *Black Mountain: An Exploration in Community*, pp. 213-215.

over Jordan, about the Gospel Feast, wouldn't that give her soul grounding in all the worlds, invisible and visible? Wouldn't it make sense that she would, in later life, find herself organizing a writing circle, focused on African-American poetry, and call it "Deep River?"

## A Band of Angels

> *Sophia...is the leavening influence of life...Wisdom connects, enlivens...She is a protecting Goddess and a hidden one...She is a Black Goddess... because she is primal.*[8]

In a lifetime of tracking dreams, I am struck by the power of black folk in white folks' dreamtime. Take me for example. When I was in a major life transition, a psychological borderland, terminating an analysis of many years, Sophia showed up in a dream as a light skinned black woman. She was preparing me for a wedding, feeding me corn, red pepper, black beans. She, whose name means wisdom, announced to me in active imagination that she would be taking over the analytic function. Indeed, she is more available than any analyst, for, as it is said in the Jewish tradition, "no sooner do you call to Wisdom than she stands ready to serve you at your gates."[9] Sophia says that her father is Greek and her mother is African. How am I to make sense of this, when I am a Jew, and she clearly comes from the Hebrew Bible, from the Book of Proverbs, where it is written?

> Doth not wisdom cry? and understanding put forth her voice?
> She standeth in the top of high places...
> She crieth at the gates, at the entry of the city....[10]

Does the Sophia who speaks for the wisdom traditions, she who is the beloved of God, come from Africa bearing the secrets of the ancient feminine? With her beautiful skin, darker than mine, lighter than her African mother, Sophia integrates races and cultures. She leads me to

---

8   Caitlin Matthews, *Sophia: Goddess of Wisdom, Bride of God*, pp. xxxi-xxxii.
9   Howard Schwartz, *The Tree of Souls: The Mythology of Judaism*, p. 45.
10  King James Bible, *Proverbs*, 8:1-3.

the "Deep River" of African American music and poetry. She is, von Franz tells us, the "wisdom of God."[11] She shape-shifts in my dreams. In a dream, I am exhausted, naked, wandering. It was a time in my life between selling a beloved home and buying a townhouse. Two dignified older black women, who remind me of the wise black sisters in Sue Monk Kidd's wonderful novel, *The Secret Life of Bees*, take care of me. In active imagination, they tell me they are sisters, Sophia and Isis. They have the same mother, Africa, but different fathers. Jung describes the connection between Isis and Sophia in *Mysterium*:

> ...the cognomen of Isis was...The Black One...She was also called the Old One...She appears as a teacher of alchemy in the treatise "Isis the Prophetess to her son Horus"...She...was equated with Sophia.[12]

Isis is *prima materia*, mystery of the natural world, the philosophical stone, the mystery of the widow, she to whom the angel, who desires her, gives the secrets of alchemy, according to von Franz.[13] She is the Lady of Healing, source of medicinal herbs, great sorceress.[14] The black ones, the old ones, the wise ones, Isis and Sophia are my travelling companions, part of the band of angels of African origin, who guide my inner life. Perhaps they were among the fairies at my cradle.

But it's not just women in that band of angels. When did I dream of that black man, wearing a fedora? That hat is always a giveaway that the dream refers to my childhood, when men like my father wore those fine-looking hats. The man in my dream was solid, comforting. I knew him to be the uncle of a wild and troubled man-child; he was the only one who could contain him. How long has he been dreaming in me, wanting to be let out? It's clear to me now that he carries the energy of Roland Hayes. Sixty years after I met him, I long to reach back to Roland Hayes, to talk to him, to hear his living voice, to listen to his stories.

---

11  Marie-Louise von Franz, *Alchemy*, p. 136.
12  Jung, "The Components of the Coniunctio," *Mysterium*, CW 14, ¶ 14.
13  von Franz, *Alchemy*, p. 52.
14  Shirley Nicholson, *The Goddess Re-Awakening*, p. 91.

## My Soul is a Witness

> *In characteristic and picturesque pattern, the narrator in "A Witness" summons prophets of both Old and New Testaments. Knitting them together, he presents...the oneness of Truth.*[15]

In his day, everybody knew the story of Roland Hayes, the son of poor tenant farmers, former slaves, who became a world famous tenor and sang before the crowned heads of Europe. But it is long past his day, and it is hard to find his music or stories about his life. I did find a biography written by his friend, MacKinley Helm, in Hayes' voice. It is called, *Angel Mo and her Son, Roland Hayes*, and was published in the 40s. I also found a songbook called, *My Favorite Spirituals*, arranged and interpreted by Roland Hayes. I think we had that songbook when I was a child. And, to my delight, I learned of a new biography as I was gathering this collection. Finally, we have a fitting tribute to this great singer, the musicologically sophisticated *Roland Hayes: The Legacy of an America Tenor*, by Christopher A. Brooks and Robert Sims, published in 2015.

Roland Hayes was born in 1887. His father claimed to be part Cherokee and much preferred the woods to the farm. In the words his biographer puts in his mouth, Hayes says:

> He taught me to identify the songs of birds...I used to stop work in the fields to listen to meadow larks, orchard orioles and summer tanagers—fancying, in the sympathetic way I learned from my father, that I was a bird addressed by my companions in the trees, and birdlike answering them.
>
> When my father called a deer, he was a buck himself...He made an offering of his whole nature...He opened the way for me to become a musician by showing me how to offer my body...to receive the music which he taught me to discover in the natural world. I learned from my father how the body follows the imagination.[16]

---

15  Hayes, *My Favorite Spirituals*, p. 47.
16  MacKinley Helm, *Angel Mo' and Her Son, Roland Hayes*, pp. 11-12.

He says of his mother:

> My mother was a small, slight woman, with a beautiful erect carriage which hard work never bent. She was very little more than five feet tall, and she moved rapidly about on her small feet, quick and sprightly as a bird.[17]

> Mother...worked hard all her life. She plowed and hoed and picked cotton. She washed and ironed for the white families... who kept the store and owned the sawmill and gristmill...[18]

Roland lost his father when he was eleven, and soon thereafter the family moved away from the farm to the city of Chattanooga. His mother took in washing, and Roland found work at a foundry. He nearly lost his life in that foundry, when he fell into a conveyor belt and was pulled into a machine that crushed and mangled him.[19] His survival was miraculous.

So was the series of events that led to his ascent unto the world stage. He had begun singing in the black church where his beautiful voice was recognized and he learned the music of his people. Word about his gift got out in the community and he was asked to sing for a graduation ceremony at his school. Professor Calhoun from Oberlin Conservatory of Music happened to be there and was so impressed with Hayes' voice that he offered to give him singing lessons for 50 cents a lesson. Hayes' mother, who insisted that all her children be educated, and wanted Roland to become a preacher, thought it a waste of money. No black man could expect a future as a singer. Nevertheless, Hayes started studying with Calhoun. Calhoun played a recording of Caruso singing and Hayes was transported. He wanted to sing like that. He went on to Fisk University where he joined the Jubilee Singers, renowned for bringing black religious music to a wider audience. When the Jubilee Singers traveled to Boston, Hayes went with them and stayed there, determined to find a teacher. He was accepted as a scholarship student by Arthur Hubbard,

---

17  Helm, *Angel Mo' and Her Son, Roland Hayes*, p. 51.
18  Helm, *Angel Mo' and Her Son, Roland Hayes*, p. 47.
19  Robert C. Hayden, *Singing for All People*, p. 12.

who began training him in the European repertoire, and encouraged him to go to Europe, where "it was no crime to be black."[20]

Hayes sailed to England, where he slowly built up so fine a reputation that he was invited to sing for the King and Queen. He sang the classical repertoire, but he also sang spirituals. He made a great impression on Queen Mary and with her help his career took off. On the Continent in 1924, he was scheduled to sing for a German audience. He had been warned that there might be trouble. He saw an open letter in the morning newspaper, warning of the "calamity" of an American Negro, "who had come to Berlin to defile the names of German poets and composers, a Negro…who, at best, could only remind us of the cotton fields of Georgia."[21] His new biography describes the difficult drama of facing a hostile audience as Roland Hayes and his accompanist on the piano, William Lawrence, walked onto a dark stage before the Berlin house, filled to its 1,000-seat capacity.

> Roland and Lawrence…took their respective positions in a single spotlight aimed at where the tenor was to stand, as if he were somehow a target. When he made it to the bend of the piano, he began hearing faint hisses. Over the course of a minute they grew louder and louder. The "barrage" of protest continued for close to ten minutes while Roland stood perfectly still with his eyes closed and his head upright… In his mind he uttered his standard prayer while facing an audience…."God, please blot out Roland Hayes so that the people will see only thee." [22]

Hayes chose to begin with Schubert's "Du Bist die Ruh," slowly, in a "barely audible pianissimo."[23] He sang that gorgeous prayer invoking calm, peace and longing, and "only in the final climactic section…did Roland, give more volume,"[24] soaring above the accompaniment, before returning to his "stunningly effective pianissimo."

---

20   Helm, *Angel Mo' and Her Son, Roland Hayes*, p. 151.
21   Helm, *Angel Mo' and Her Son, Roland Hayes*, p, 21.
22   Christopher A. Brooks and Robert Sims, *Roland Hayes*, pp. 121-2.
23   Brooks and Sims, *Roland Hayes*, p. 122.
24   Brooks and Sims, *Roland Hayes*, p. 123.

At the close of the performance, there was total silence throughout the house. In his heart and psyche, Roland knew that the performance had transformed the audience's disdain into respect, if not admiration, for him and his artistry. Only then did he slowly open his eyes. The spirit *had* done its work.[25]

Hayes was able to turn his European success into an opening in his own country. He made his debut at Town Hall in December 1923, singing both classical works and spirituals. The *New York World* columnist, Heywood Broun wrote of the event:

> Roland Hayes sang of Jesus…and it seemed to me that this was what religion ought to be, it was a mood rather than a creed, an emotion rather than a doctrine…I saw a miracle at Town Hall. Half of the people were black and half were white and while the mood of the song held, they were all the same. They shared together the close silence. One emotion wrapped them. And at the end it was a single sob.[26]

Hayes was bridging a wide cultural gap in bringing the European classical tradition together with black religious music. This is illustrated by an incident early in his career when he was on an obscure tour to the west coast, and his mother was traveling with him. Though he usually sang in black churches he had been invited to sing at a benefit for a white congregation in Santa Monica. He sang the spiritual, "My Soul is a Witness."

> It seemed to be making very little impression upon my well-groomed white audience. Of the whole company of people there, only my mother was a practitioner of the primitive and highly emotional religion which had produced those sermons in song; and she, great soul, under the compulsion of deep religious feeling, stood up in the midst of that fashionable assembly and called out, in a clear and ringing voice, "Hallelujah! I'm a witness too."

---

25  Brooks and Sims, *Roland Hayes*, p. 123.
26  Helm, *Angel Mo' and Her Son, Roland Hayes*, p. 188.

> It was as though she had touched a match to a resinous torch. The hall became suddenly luminous, with the light of feeling come out of its dark hiding place, and at the end there was a fury of applause…[27]

After the concert Hayes was approached by a white man who spoke to him about the quality of his voice, a quality not found in white singers. Hayes had to recognize that he "had been working in a cloud of depression because my voice had not come out as white as…I…hoped it would."[28] He described a great relief of inner tension when he recognized that he could be what no white artist could be.

## Swing Low, Sweet Chariot

> *Ask the Sophia within…*[29]

As we approach the last portion of our days, we are called by the first of our days, called by the fairies who gathered around our cradle. "What did you do with that gift I gave you?" What did I do with the blessing I was given, in the person of Roland Hayes?

Why is Roland Hayes so powerful for me? As the black uncle in the fedora in my dream, he is the only one who can contain his restless unfocused nephew. Does the bad boy in me settle down in his presence, like that German audience did? Is he a reconciling figure, bringing together the oppositional forces in me that might otherwise battle it out: the European vs. the American, Mozart and Bach vs. spirituals and blues, high brow vs. low brow, religious attitude vs. worldly drive?

Did I sit in his lap as a toddler? Did I hear him tell his stories? What would I ask him— were some good fairy to come along and grant me this wish? Suddenly I realize, Sophia is with me—my inner analyst—a dark inquiring presence, with beautiful skin and an irritated edge.

---

27  Helm, *Angel Mo' and Her Son, Roland Hayes*, pp. 122-3.
28  Helm, *Angel Mo' and Her Son, Roland Hayes*, p. 123.
29  von Franz, *Alchemy*, p. 136.

*Some good fairy? Who do you suppose I am? Why don't you remember to call on me when you need me? You are trying to do something very important, you are calling up an ancestor. You need me.*

Calling up an ancestor? Is that what I'm doing? Is Roland Hayes my ancestor?

*There are ancestors of the blood and ancestors of the soul. Some are both. They live in the world tree and wait to be released by a mortal who knows their power. When they are brought into consciousness by the living, spoken to, written to, fed, they can ensure a flood of "radiant blessings"[30] from the invisible world. Roland Hayes has been mostly forgotten. But as you say, he is a shining spirit, a luminous light. You need him. Your world needs him. Call him up from the dead, tell him who you are.*

Sophia has a way of turning an offhand remark into a major project. I am a little nervous, but, here goes:

"Mr. Hayes, I am Eddie Lowinsky's daughter, that towheaded two-year-old, toddling about when you came to Black Mountain College in the summer of 1945. Do you remember? You are long gone, and sadly not remembered for the trailblazer you were. I call you from the Promised Land, the campground, the Gospel Feast where all is peace. I call you from your home over Jordan. You've been pulling at me so intensely. Are you trying to get my attention?"

I see that Sophia, with her beautiful skin and dark eyes, has shape-shifted into a large male presence in a fedora. He sits as if on a stairway, or a front porch. In life, he was a small delicate man. As a ghost, he is large, encompassing, warm—a warm ghost, strange as that sounds, with a bright spirit. I can see him shining.

*Ah child,* he says, *we dead are always looking for a channel through to the living. You are your father's daughter in your love for words and their music. But there's something else in you, something to which your father paid little mind, though it was the content of the music he studied: strong religious feeling, spiritual longing. You heard it in Gregorian chant, in the masses of Palestrina and of Bach, and in the spirituals I sang in your home when you were a child.*

---

30 Stephen Karcher, "Re-enchanting the Mind," *Psychological Perspectives*, Vol. 50, #2, p. 207.

*Is there anybody listening to these songs now, outside the black church? I poured my passion for this music into my life. Is there anyone who appreciates the great religious vision of my people? The dead want to feel their work go on. Some of us dead make our peace over Jordan. Some of us dead don't. We're restless. Our business in the realm of humans is unfinished. What I need, for my soul to rest, is for the wisdom of my people, the wisdom of God as expressed in spirituals, to be heard.*

I feel the deep rich energy of Roland Hayes' personality. I feel held by him. Something restless and troubled in me settles down. I want him to keep on talking with that kindness of his—that cultured intelligence. Wisdom he says, the wisdom of God. He is talking about Sophia—he is talking about my inner guide.

Mr. Hayes, tell me about the wisdom of God as expressed in spirituals. You studied them, arranged them for solo voice and piano. You know, I have an inner figure named Sophia. She comes to me in dreams and in active imagination. She was just here, advising me to invoke you. She is the wisdom of God. She tells me her mother is Africa. I've never quite understood that, since my people are Jews. Do spirituals come from Africa? Or are they the music of slaves submitting to their master's religion?

*Ah, you have an African spirit guide. No wonder you've been able to invoke me. No wonder your soul needs to carry my light on. Africa is the mother of us all, our spiritual home. Hers is a wisdom that can take in the gods of other traditions while holding onto her own ancestral traditions. That's what the spirituals did. My mother, who was born a slave, told me: "The master, yes, one had to acknowledge him, I belonged to him, it was the law of the land... but what I am, here inside me, he couldn't touch."* [31] *That's the great dignity, the amazing wisdom of these songs. They are rooted in Africa; they reach back to Africa's rhythms, her great "Mother Drum," they evoke some high frequency vibration familiar to Africans that harmonizes nature, God, and people; they improvise on African "call and response" while borrowing from the white man's hymnal. They give instruction, by*

---

31 Hayes, *My Favorite Spirituals*, pp. 93-4.

*allegory, as was the custom among our ancestors, which made it easy for us to translate our religious experience into the stories of the white man's Bible.*[32]

*I translated these songs for the concert hall, for solo voice and piano. Originally, they had been sung by unaccompanied chorus, by slaves working in the fields. In those days they were our lifeblood, how we cultivated our souls and our community, while keeping the master off our backs. Slave owners encouraged singing. It helped them keep track of their human property. They got more work out of their slaves when they sang.*

*We looked like we were cultivating the fields, and so we were. But at the same time, we were transmitting subversive messages about secret revival meetings, or about the way to freedom. The spiritual "Follow the Drinking Gourd" gives directions by starlight to the runaway slave heading north. "Steal Away," a favorite of mine, was on one level the announcement of a religious revival meeting. Imagine a cotton field where there are many slaves hoeing cotton. The leader has arranged for a clergyman from the North to preach the gospel secretly after nightfall. He whispers, "Steal Away" to the slave next in line to him. This whispered word, spoken over rhythmic measures of hoe strokes is passed along the line until it reaches the last individual. Work takes on a livelier gait. The spoken word takes on melody, which surges forth on the rhythmic verve of an African idiomatic patter. The hoes simply play an ecstatic rhythm as a background to the song. The plan of the slaves to attend the religious services secretly, after nightfall, is hidden from the master.*[33]

*Imagine what it was like in that cotton field. I know something about that. We were tenant farmers when I was a child. Imagine the heat of the sun beating down on our heads and our aching backs, the nasty way the cotton bolls cut our hands, our tired feet. And then the rhythm that carried our resistance, our tenacity, our heritage. Drums were forbidden in many areas. They frightened the overseers. They carried our old African power, our forbidden gods. But we didn't need drums. We had hands to clap, feet to stomp, hoes to strike the ground.*[34]

Roland Hayes bright spirit seems to flicker, to fill up with a question.

---

32  Hayes, *My Favorite Spirituals*, pp. 10-13.
33  Hayes, *My Favorite Spirituals*, p. 74.
34  Eileen Southern, *The Music of Black Americans*, p. 195.

*Child, do you have another spirit guide besides Sophia? There's someone else nudging me. Calls herself Isis. She's angry, says she's being neglected.*

Yes, Isis is a spirit guide. I don't know what she wants. Isn't one inner analyst enough? I thought she and Sophia were interchangeable.

The spirit of Hayes has disappeared. A dark female spirit emerges with fierce eyes that glow like a cat's. She says:

*Sophia and I are not interchangeable! I'm a lot older and a lot crankier. You call on Sophia when you want clarity, wisdom, perspective. But I'm the one who tracks you in the invisible realms and I have an agenda! I'm more priestess than analyst. I'm the one who insists you make something of your feelings, your dreams, your inner experiences. I'm the one who insists you make poems. I'm the one that makes things real. It's not enough to call up an ancestor and have a nice conversation. You need to feed the brother!*

Isis is clearly frustrated with me.

How do I feed a ghost?

*That's obvious. Feed him a poem!*

Do you mean the poem I wrote about my experience at Black Mountain?

*For one.*

### Mae West Is What They Called Your Hills

>back in Black Mountain College days;
>your great green breasts made glad
>my baby years. Your willows, your maples, whispered all
>
>the secrets of the sexual earth. You love goddess,
>you come hither and yon, hitchhiker to the bottom
>of Lake Eden, big wind over moving waters, you who
>
>leap from mountain ridge to mountain ridge, who break
>the vessels and the rules; make a man hard, a woman wet,
>a little girl full of dreamy meanderings. O queen
>
>of the purple flower, music was made between your thighs,
>fiery as Mozart, tender as Beethoven, melancholy

as the spirituals sung by Roland Hayes—first black man

at a white southern college—in that dining hall in 1945. But you,
gorgeous and terrible, who knew the parts
my mother didn't play, the ones my father disapproved,

have broken the world into pieces. Some say
you were a free spirit, a wild adventurer; some say
you were a danger to us all, a harlot, a slut.

You ate the apple, made the snake dance,
had us cast out of paradise. And so you did,
and so we were, Mae West.    But I
                          remain

                your
                priestess.[35]

Isis' cat eyes are gone, and it's Roland Hayes again. If a ghost's eyes can twinkle, Roland Hayes' do.

*Black Mountain was a pretty sexy place, though I understand that caused some trouble. How good to be written into the world of your poem, next to Mozart and Beethoven.*

You know, I'd like to feed you another poem, one I wrote under the influence of Al Young. His poems are influenced by the blues. He's a musician himself. He wrote a wonderful poem called, "A Dance for Ma Rainey."

*You mean the famous "Mother of the Blues," the one credited with naming the form? Asks the spirit of Roland Hayes.*

The very one. Here's the beginning of Al's poem, which is like a long musical riff.

        I'm going to be just like you, Ma
        Rainey this monday morning
        clouds puffing up out of my head
        like those balloons

---

35   Lowinsky, first published in *Texas Review.*

that float above the faces of white people
in the funnypaper

I'm going to hover in the corners
of the world, Ma
& sing from the bottom of hell
up to the tops of high heaven
& send out scratchless waves of yellow
& brown & that basic black honey
misery

I'm going to cry so sweet
& so low
& so dangerous
Ma,
that the message is going to reach you
back in 1922
where you shimmer
snaggle-toothed
perfumed &
powdered
in your bauble beads[36]

The spirit of Roland Hayes lights up. He says: *He makes it sound so simple, but I suspect it's not at all simple, the way he covers the entire realm of African-American experience: saying he's going to "sing from the bottom of hell/up to the tops of high heaven." That about says it for spirituals, for blues, for jazz. And when he says he's going to send his cry back to Ma Rainey in 1922, that puts me in mind of your spirit guide Sophia, talking to you about "fixing an ancestor." I think that's what he's doing. Am I right Sophia?*

She appears, my inner analyst, she of the beautiful skin and the deep calm, saying: *I thank you for not forgetting me. Yes, Young is fixing an ancestor in that poem. He is naming his lineage, that the great mother of his poetry is Ma Rainey, in her terrible suffering, in her amazing music.*

---

36  Al Young, *Heaven: Collected Poems, 1956-1990*, pp. 18-19.

She turns to me, with her lovely smile. *Your poem in response to Young fixes your musical ancestry. Why don't you read it?*

## Your People Are My People

>    for Al Young

My people are the people of the pianoforte and the violin
Mozart people   Bach people   Hallelujah people
My people are the Requiem people   Winterreise people
Messiah people   who crossed the red sea   Pharoah's dogs
>                                              at our heels

Your people are the drum beat people   the field holler
people  the conjure people   Blues people  Jubilee people  people who talk
straight to God    Your people are the Old Man River people
the Drinking Gourd people   singing the Lord's song
>                                        in a strange land

My family had a Sabbath ritual
We lit the candles sang Go Down Moses   sang Swing Low
Sweet Chariot   sang slave music freedom music secret signals
in the night music    My father said you never know
>                              when Pharoah will be back

I was young
I was American   I thought
my people were the Beatles   the Lovin' Spoonful   the Jefferson
Airplane  singing Alice and her White Rabbit through all
>                     those changes my parents did not understand

That didn't last
That was leaving home music   magic mushroom music
Puff the Dragon music  floating off
to Never Never land   now heard in elevators
>                                in the pyramids of finance

But Old Man River still rolls through my fields
Bessie Smith still sweetens my bowl
Ma Rainey appears in the inner sanctum
of the CG Jung Institute   flaunting her deep black bottom

My father's long gone over Jordan
and I'd hate for him to see
how right he was about Pharoah

but I want you to know     Al

every Christmas
in black churches all over Chicago
the Messiah shows up
accompanied by my mother's
        Hallelujah violin![37]

*Ah child,* says the ghost of Roland Hayes, *now I feel nourished.*

So, as you can see, my story has changed. I am not only the child of catastrophe. I am also the child of a fertile borderland between the old world and the new, gifted by fairies, witness to a transformative moment of desegregation, which my parents facilitated. I live in a version of this "Home Over Jordan" to this day, where landscape is the Great Goddess, where the visible and invisible worlds meet, where poetry begins, where a band of angels. Isis, Sophia, and now Roland Hayes, guides my way.

---

37  Lowinsky, first published in *New Millennium Writings.*

## Chapter 6

## History is a Ghost Story
## Reflections on South Africa, Collective Trauma, and the Uses of Poetry[1]

> *It is only after a faithful journey to a distant region, a foreign country, or strange land, that the meaning of the inner voice that is to guide our quest can be revealed to us.*[2]

### Escorted by Ghosts

> *We were born to escort the dead, and be escorted ourselves.*[3]

*History is a ghost story. We tell it to each other around the fire; it scares us.*

   I was "born to escort the dead." My ghosts are always with me. They gather to mutter about danger, to lament what happened, to remind me where I come from. They fill up my notebooks, take over my poems, demand their stories be told. Sometimes it feels like an obsession, sometimes I feel it as my life work—to express the trauma of my people—the

---

1  Lowinsky, first published in an earlier form in *Psychological Perspectives*, Volume 54, Issue 4.
2  Heinrich Zimmer, *Myths and Symbols in Indian Art and Civilization*, p. 221.
3  Charles Wright, *A Short History of the Shadow*, p. 9.

Shoah—and find despite it, within it, because of it—a relationship to the divine.

The ghosts of my grandmothers are major players in my psyche. They show up often. But when I had the opportunity to travel to South Africa it was the ghost of my father that insisted on traveling with me. My father was a difficult parent—critical, domineering; the world of my childhood revolved around fear of him. But he was also brilliant, highly educated, a scholar of musical history and the arts, and passionate about political life. In 1933 he was working on his dissertation at Heidelberg when the danger to Jews began to escalate.

His family lived in Stuttgart. They were warned by a policeman, who was not a Jew, that they should flee. My father wrote his dissertation in 40 days, and then stole across the border to Holland in the night. He was an illegal alien. Had he been caught, he might have been sent back to Germany and shot. It happened that his dissertation, which is still controversial in musicological circles, was called, "Secret Chromatic Art in the Netherlands Motet." In one of those transformation tales, those miracle stories one hears from émigrés, my father met Queen Juliana of Holland, told her about his work, and ended up becoming the piano teacher to her daughter, the princess.

My father has been gone for many years. But in recent years he's been haunting me, demanding that I honor his strong spirit, that I claim him in my being.

*History is a ghost—a hungry ghost. It haunts us, shaping our experience in the image of the past. We think we are in the familiar terrible story. But what if it's a different story that is unfolding?*

"Narrative arises with the recognition that we are bearers of history… embedded in the various traditions we inherit and transform," says the poet Alan Shapiro.[4] The tradition I've inherited is what Jungian analyst Samuel Kimbles calls a "phantom narrative"[5]—a ghost story shaped by collective trauma, which shapes experience, as though it were the only truth. We Jews, especially those of us with an immediate link to the Shoah, inhabit a double realm. There is the realm of the good life many

---

4  Quoted in Tony Hoagland, *Real Sofistikashun,* p. 170.
5  Samuel Kimbles, *Phantom Narratives.*

of us have been lucky to lead; there is the realm of terror, just below the surface, where the ghost of my father keeps scanning the horizons for Hitler, for the return of Pharaoh, for the next catastrophe. During the years of the Bush imperial presidency, I kept hearing his voice filled with dread, horrified by torture, surveillance, secrecy—all signs of incipient fascism, he told me. My father taught me the uses of poetry by the way he used music. He was an accomplished pianist, and the passion he poured into Bach and Chopin gave me a great gift: I understood how art could become a transformative vessel for deep inchoate feeling. I could not talk directly to my father about anything emotional. But I could listen to him pour his suffering, his struggle, his longing into a Bach fugue, a Chopin etude, and gather from that a major use of my own poetry.

I surprised myself a few years ago, by writing a villanelle— a very structured poetic form which derives originally from an Italian folk song. It honors two vital ghosts: my father and my maternal grandmother.

## Adagio and Lamentation

>When my father's fierce fingers made Bach flow
>our dead came in and sat with us   a ghostly visitation
>and my grandmother sang lieder   in memory of long ago
>
>This is how prayer was said in my childhood   solo
>piano   arguing with god   adagio and  lamentation
>when my father's fierce fingers made Bach flow
>
>Music accompanied us into the valley of the shadow and lo
>Bach was Torah   Mozart was our rod   Schubert led us into
>                                                   contemplation
>My grandmother sang lieder   remembering long-ago
>
>My child's soul was full of glimmerings   the glamour of the gone
>                                                   the glow
>of candles borne by children into the dark German woods
>                                                   the illumination
>of the evergreen   all this I saw and more   when my father's
>          fierce fingers made Bach flow

My mother's dead sister   my grandfather in a cattle car   Woe
permeated shadows   stirred the curtains   took up habitation
in my grandmother's body   filled every song she sang   with how
                                                    she longed for long ago

long gone now   my grandmother   my father   although
sometimes I call them back   by villanelle   by incantation
Come my fierce father   play for me   water my soul in Bach's flow
Sing my sad grandmother   your song is my covenant with long   ago"[6]

The poet Tony Hoagland writes: "Modern consciousness may indeed be splintered, but it is one function of poetry in our time to fasten it back together…"[7] Writing this poem helped fasten me back together. I don't usually write formal poems, and I seldom write poems with end rhymes. But poems have minds of their own, and this poem insisted on form and rhyme. Imposing that level of order on the chaos of thronging ghosts that invades my psyche helped me contain overwhelming collective trauma. My father was a secular Jew, a cultural Jew. He did not, consciously, have a religious attitude. But in the writing of the poem the obvious was revealed—the religion I grew up in was music. I had a visceral and transformative experience of the divine when my father played the piano, and when my grandmother sang.

*History is a con artist, a heart breaker, a smasher of destinies.*

I belong to the moment, 76 years ago, when my father crossed the border into Holland in the night. I belong to the moment, in the first stirring of the cells that became me, when my father's mother died in the concentration camp, Lag Westerbork, wondering whether her daughter-in-law might be pregnant. My psyche was formed around the question: How does one recover from collective trauma?

Early in my life, the answer seemed clear: "Never Again!" It was my father's answer—one fights against prejudice and discrimination; one works for desegregation; one supports the state of Israel; one belongs to the ACLU; one writes to one's congressman; one is eternally vigilant. That clarity did not last long. I remember standing in the newspaper

---

6  Lowinsky, first published in *Atlanta Review.*
7  Tony Hoagland, *Real Sofistikashun,* p. 171.

office next door to my home in Hyderabad, India. It was 1968. My then husband was the Peace Corps doctor. As usual, we had a group of Peace Corps volunteers at our house for lunch. As usual, we were talking politics. We were fiercely against the Vietnam War. We were angry with Lyndon Johnson.

Word came to us around the lunch table of the assassination of Martin Luther King. We all ran next door to watch the ticker tape. The Indian journalists, our Hyderabadi neighbors, our servants, all wept with us. They knew Martin Luther King was our Gandhi. They understood our trauma through their own. I found myself in a world where things were not getting better, people were not less violent, not more open minded…

## Do You Remember Africa?

> *Do you remember Africa?*
> *O cleave the air fly away home*
> *My gran, he flew back to Africa,*
> *Just spread his arms and*
>             *Flew away home.*[8]

*History is a heavy load; we carry it on our shoulders, we load it on our donkeys, on the backs of our children, walking slowly to the new world.*

When the Jungians decided to have their International Meeting in South Africa, the ghost of my father began lobbying in my soul. His spirit in me was stirred. He reminded me that our family had always identified with black people, beginning with the great tenor, Roland Hayes who brought spirituals to the concert hall, and whom my father had invited to sing at Black Mountain College in North Carolina, to an integrated audience in 1945. Spirituals carried the seeds of African culture and kept the spirits of black folk alive during the terrible times of slavery. The spirit of my father reminded me that it was his idea that we should sing spirituals as part of our Sabbath ritual, when I was a

---

8  Robert Hayden, "O Daedalus Fly Away Home," *Collected Poems,* p. 55.

child. (You've noticed, perhaps, how my father is always the hero of these stories?)

I had spent two years with the Deep River writing circle I lead at the San Francisco Jung Institute reading African American poetry, and writing under its influence. That was soul food. And it revealed to me my own longing for Africa. Africa is origin, motherland, "Our Home Over Jordan,"—the place one flies away to on the wings of imagination as in Robert Hayden's poem "O Daedalus, Fly Away Home"—Africa is all of our ancestral home, the place we all began. Audre Lorde writes:

> Seboulisa mother goddess with one breast
> Eaten away by worms of sorrow and loss
> See me now
> Your severed daughter[9]

I understood that I too, am a "severed daughter" of the African goddess.

It is not always peaceful between my father's spirit and my own. We do not worship the same gods. I can hear his familiar hectoring tone in my head, full of his certainties, blind to my feelings. He says, *All that goddess stuff you spout is intellectual rubbish. There's no proof that matriarchal societies existed and if they did they were illiterate and without culture! You have too fine a mind to buy into such superstitious nonsense!*

Am I going to allow this negative spirit to hitch a ride with me to Africa?

Mostly, my ghosts are benign. They guide me; they show me lost worlds; they orient my soul. My father's ghost can be inspiring; he can fill me with passion for the great questions of my time. But often he is a troublemaker. His words trick and trap me into some version of myself that has nothing to do with who I am.

Once, long ago when I was in my thirties, a life crisis took the form of a serious illness—high fevers, death in the form of a big yellow blob on my bed. I performed an act of violence in my imagination: I tore my

---

9   Audre Lorde, "125th Street and Abomey," *The Collected Poems of Audre Lorde*, p. 241.

father's face to shreds, I tore up his dominating tongue, his mesmer eyes, his ability to fascinate me out of my own skin. I needed to rip him up to claim my own life, but it horrified me. It still does.

My father was alive then, but I had to murder his power over me. Though he is dead, he still has too much power. Is this a ghost with whom I can have a conversation? Or would I have to burn up the memory of his spell?

Does that mean I've not forgiven him? Does forgiveness mean accepting what was crippling? I know how bound up he was, caught in undigested terrors of Nazis and Cossacks. Is it possible to transform a culture complex? If I took my father with me to a place where myth had become history—where ancient troubles had shifted and people had begun to make a difference, would he change in me?

Like my father, I am a citizen of the world; like him, I care passionately about what happens in far away lands. We watched in horror as black Africans were severed from whites, made to live in townships outside of the town, severed from the power, the education, the wealth of their own land. We'd seen Mandela jailed, Stephen Biko brutally murdered. My father had not lived to see Mandela walk out of prison, had not lived to experience the new world Bishop Tutu describes on April 27th, 1994—election day in South Africa:

*History is a healer, a creator of new life, a giver of joy.*

> The day for which we had waited all these many long years, the day for which the struggle against apartheid had been waged, for which so many of our people had been tear gassed, bitten by police dogs, struck with quirts and batons, for which many more had been detained, tortured and banned, for which others had gone into exile—the day had finally dawned when we…could vote for the first time…I was sixty-two years old before I could vote. Nelson Mandela was seventy-six…[10]
>
> It was a veritable spiritual experience. It was a mountaintop experience. The black person entered the booth one person and emerged on the other side a new transfigured person. She

---

10  Desmond Tutu, *No Future Without Forgiveness*, p. 3.

entered weighed down by the anguish and burden of oppression, with the memory of being treated like rubbish gnawing away at her vitals like some corrosive acid. She reappeared as someone new, "I am free," as she walked away with her head held high…and an elastic spring in her step.[11]

I realized that it wasn't only that the spirit of my father needed to experience this new world through me, but that I needed his fierce light, his luminous presence as part of my own spirit.

## Most Stony South African God

> *who's that rowing a black boat*
> *black in the black night?*
> *who's that hearing the slavebell*
> *and beating the thud of his gut?*[12]

*History is a trickster, a thief. It cheats us out of where we think we're going, what we think we own, whom we love.*

On the day we arrived in South Africa in a jet-lagged haze, we were told we had to go to the mountain. This was Table Mountain, an imposing flat-topped stony god that presides over Cape Town. It was a clear bright day. There was no "table cloth," no cluster of clouds hanging over the mountain, obscuring the view. This, we were told, was most unusual—coming after days of rain—an opportunity we had to seize. So we found ourselves on top of the world, glorying in views of the wild coast, Devil's Peak, the Twelve Apostles. We meandered in a strange marshland filled with wildflowers. A bright green-necked, orange-breasted bird flew by. I had not understood how much of the magnetic pull of Africa comes from the landscape. In Cape Town, everywhere you go the mountain dominates—pulls your eyes, your mind, from the business of the street to the high slow language of rocks and earth.

---

11  Tutu, *No Future Without Forgiveness*, p. 7.
12  Wopko Jensma, "Cry Me a River," in *The Lava of this Land*, Denis Hirson, editor, p. 63.

It was August, 2007. We were living in the shadow of the Bush years—had no idea as yet that we were soon to have an African-American president. We felt ashamed of our own country. At the opening reception to the conference, I met Mamphela Ramphele—a tall elegant woman in black, something lacy at her throat. She embodies South African history. In her youth, she and her lover, Stephen Biko, were among the founders of the Black Consciousness movement of the 70s. I had read about them, read the poetry of that time. In the new South Africa, she became the Vice Chancellor of the University of Cape Town—the first black woman to hold such a position at a South African University—and a Managing Director of the World Bank.

My father's spirit leapt and glowed—he had always loved beautiful women, was a master of seduction. Was it he in me who went on and on to her about what a beacon South Africa was to our country? Martin Luther King and Malcolm X had been assassinated—leaving us without meaning and direction. South Africa had changed so dramatically for the better. It was an inspiration.

Was it the spirit of my father to which she responded, saying that my people were her inspiration, for the Jews had always valued literacy and education? That's what the new South Africa needs. My father loves that kind of talk. I had been reading South African poetry, poems that told the unbearable stories. We spoke of Mongane Wally Serote and his long poem, "Freedom Lament and Song":

> the history of my continent
> it begins
> it repeats
> it starts
> after the crack of the sun
> after the secret burials
> after the smell of burnt flesh
> it starts...
>
> i
> i am here look at me nice

i survived Vlakplaas[13]

Vlakplaas was a farm near Pretoria, used as a base for police hit squads during apartheid. It became a symbol of brutality.

On the next day, Ramphele was our plenary speaker. She wore a bright red dress and shawl and shone throughout the hall. She was bold and her manner was fierce, her vision wide and political. She spoke of the Truth and Reconciliation Commission, which had been established by the post-Apartheid government to facilitate recovery of the truth of what had happened. Hearings were held in public. She described it as a ritual of healing that helped the country find meaning. She spoke of its limitations, its failures. She spoke of the social engineering of apartheid, which destroyed families by separating the men, forcing them to live in barracks away from wives and children. Apartheid also blocked the education of young blacks, and the country was still suffering the consequences of a lost generation.

I felt touched by a world of experience I couldn't articulate—but which moved me deeply. We began to lose our innocence, the spirit of my father and I, listening to her. We had wanted to believe that a new paradigm of justice and humanity was born out of Africa, and would lead us into the Promised Land. We wanted to believe that Mandela was Moses. It's true he had walked out of prison because of his own great spirit and the wisdom and courage of then South African president F.W. de Klerk. Mandela had been elected president, there had not been bloodshed, but, as Mamphela told us, the terrible problems of economic inequality had not been solved. Whites still lived in privilege while many Black Africans were stuck in unbearable poverty. Whites complained that their children could not get work. Their talents were getting lost because they were emigrating.

Next morning, we rose early to go to Robben Island where Mandela had been in prison for 27 years. It was a choppy ride over—the Sea Princess slapping the waves—passengers going "Ooooh" as though we were on an amusement ride. In the maximum-security prison, we sat around on benches—a scraggly bunch of tourists with cameras and

---

13  Mongane Wally Serote, *Freedom, Lament and Song*, p. 43.

babies, held in a large communal cell. Our guide had spent five and a half years imprisoned here in the 80s and early 90s, for struggling against the regime. A thin, intense, sad man, whom I'll call William, he made it painfully clear he did not want to be there, still in this prison, showing tourists his painful past. After the end of apartheid, there were not enough government jobs for all the former prisoners. He came, he told us, from the poorest of the poor. His only option was this job. It was, he said, another prison sentence. He'd been here for five years and five years was too much.

Babies gurgled, sang, cried, as William spoke of Mandela's experience, and that of the prisoners in the early years—the 60s and 70s—whose deprivation and forced labor had been much more severe. But Mandela and his peers were not with us. William was. His fragility, his sweet, lost soul swept over us like a tired wind. Most of us were psychotherapists, and we were distressed to hear that William had not gotten the psychological counseling he'd requested.

"Do you accept tips?" asked Medria, a fiery spirit.

"I don't ask for them, but I accept them."

"Hear that everyone? You over there with the camera. You can't take and not give back."

Medria was naming our dilemma: were we voyeurs of human suffering? Or were we witnesses to an important historical period. In either case, William did well in tips that morning. And when Medria told him that we were a group of psychotherapists, he brightened and said he'd just begun seeing one. His counselor had called him this morning and told him she wanted him to check into a hospital for a few weeks. We all gave a sigh of relief.

William blessed us, hoped we'd enjoy his country. For he said, as many others would throughout our journey: "Whatever is wrong with my country, it is very beautiful."

We saw that beauty, the enormous power of the landscape, on our boat ride back—the stunning views of Table Mountain, shifting mists, the lovely wharf side scenes of Cape Town, its colorful buildings clustered by the sea—so like, so unlike, our own San Francisco. We were disoriented, our sense of things ruptured.

A group of us had lunch. Gingerly, we tried to talk about it. We compared what we were seeing to our own country. I said: If we were strangers traveling to America, and were given a tour of East Oakland, told about the life of youngsters who have seen people shot before their eyes, who can't play outside because it's too dangerous, whose fathers and uncles are in prison; if we were told how public schools in poor areas were falling into disrepair for lack of funding, how young African-Americans can't find work—would it seem very different?

*I dream I am responsible for a murder. I can't remember why I did it, or how. Will I be found out? Has the body been burnt—gotten rid of? Can I live with this guilt? I am told the victim's sister wants to talk to me.*

## Ubuntu

> *He fell from the ninth floor*
> *He hanged himself*
> *He slipped on a piece of soap while washing...*
> *He hung from the ninth floor*
> *He washed from the ninth floor while slipping*
> *He hung from a piece of soap while washing*[14]

*History takes us by surprise, takes us places we had never imagined, opens new doors.*

Pumla Gobodo-Madikizela spoke to the Jungian congress. She is softer, more psychological in the personal sense, than is Ramphele. She spoke to us of the psychology of forgiveness. How does one who had a husband, son, grandson stolen from her, tortured and murdered in the most unbearable ways, look into the eyes of the one who did this, see his humanity? How does the one who perpetrated such a horror, look into the eyes of the victim, see her humanity, the preciousness of the life that was taken, and truly say—"I'm sorry." When this happens, she told us, his humanity is returned to him, hers to her.

---

14 Chris van Wyk, "In Detention," *The Lava of This Land*, Denis Hirson, editor, pp. 140-1.

She told us the story of an Askari—a former black guerilla recruited by the apartheid security forces—asking forgiveness of the mothers of men he'd killed. In Xhosa he said: "Forgive me my parents." Pumla kept repeating the Xhosa phrase, with its click. Hearing it was much more powerful than her translation. It seemed to center us—that clicking phrase, with its deep sobbing power. One of the mothers replied, "My son, I forgive you."[15] We were all a watery mass of tears.

Gobodo-Madikizela explained: "In bearing witness, confronting their depravity and coming face-to-face with the pain and suffering they have caused victims, perpetrators are re-humanizing not only their victims whose lives were shattered by their actions, but…their own sense of humanity."[16] She described how a perpetrator could become human in the process of seeing the humanity of the other. And we, who see them as monsters, begin to see them as human, when we hear their stories and their remorse.

The spirit of my father rises up in horror. Should we cultivate empathy for the guards at Bergen-Belsen who tortured his sister Ljuba, who starved her, froze her, chopped off her toes with an axe? The Jews had already been much reproached for going passively to their deaths, for not fighting. Now they were supposed to imagine the lives and struggles of their torturers, their murderers? That would be to blast to smithereens a foundation stone of our family Weltanschauung, to betray Ljuba, my grandparents who died in Europe and my grandparents who fled to the new world, bringing my father with them. It would be to betray everything I'd learned in childhood about right and wrong. My father is off and running. He is giving his familiar lecture about the Jews great contribution to history—the concept of justice. How can there be justice, demands the spirit of my father, when murderers are forgiven, when there aren't real consequences for unforgivable actions, because some soft old women are afraid to stand up for truth and justice?

I am angry with the ghost of my father. While he was alive, I couldn't stand up to him. Now I do: Father, you are being disrespectful to those wise women. You are caught in a Eurocentric worldview. Maybe they

---

15 Pumla Gobodo-Madikizela, *Cape Town Conference Proceedings*, pp. 49-50.
16 Gobodo-Madikizela, *Cape Town Conference Proceedings*, p. 44.

know something we don't know, that if there is no reconciliation, no forgiveness, the fight will go on and on, the cycle of revenge is endless. Bishop Tutu writes of the African Weltanschauung—expressed in the word ubuntu—which, according to Tutu means, "My humanity is caught up, is inextricably bound up, in yours…" Tutu writes, "We say, 'A person is a person through other persons.' It is not, 'I think therefore I am.' It says rather: 'I am human because I belong….' To forgive is not just to be altruistic. It is the best form of self-interest."[17]

Father, I am trying to forgive you for being such a tyrant of my childhood. So, I need you to back down now, and listen. Gobodo-Madikizela is bringing us both up against the dark truth that our sense of the world is based on seeing Nazis as monsters. You, father, are expressing something I feel too—it would rupture my sense of self to understand the humanity of a Nazi, to look in his eyes, to forgive him. Trauma, she says, ruptures our senses, remakes us. So it seems to me, does forgiveness.

For once, the ghost of my father is silent.

*History is an evil sorcerer, turning gold into ashes.*

Jimmy Jinta came highly recommended as a tour guide. We hired him to take us to the township, Langa. Erel Shalit, an Israeli analyst we'd befriended at a conference in Bulgaria, and his wife Sonia, joined us. Erel and Sonia live near Tel Aviv, where they've dealt with history's evil sorcery—terrorism, war, moral complexity. Sonia told us she had grown up in Congo. When she was a child, it was a safe and loving environment for her; she felt close to black people. Now Congo is a hell realm. Langa used to be a hell realm. It is where Jimmy lived, where Pumla Gobodo-Madikizela grew up. During apartheid, he told us, 66,000 families were forcibly removed from their homes in Cape Town and required to live in the crowded townships. Since the end of apartheid, there has been much improvement. He took us to the Community Center, with its colorful mosaics. Classes about Aids prevention and ceramics were advertised. We saw a pottery studio and learned that Sonia is a potter. The children are taught to make ceramic plates, cups, and other useful objects that are sold in the markets and in stores.

---

17  Tutu, *No Future Without Forgiveness*, p. 31.

We saw a group of eight-year-old girls dressed in short gingham skirts doing an enthusiastic dance to a drum—it involved high kicking over their heads. Their faces were painted with white stars, suns, arcs and other joyous markings.

We went to the Baptist Church where we were graciously received. We sat amidst the congregation, held by their spoken aloud prayers in Xhosa and in English, held in their fervent song. We were in the presence of the mountain whose backside and Devil's Peak dominate the landscape even here. The testifying passion of the women in their gorgeous dresses, their vibrant colors, their braided hair in dramatic styles, moved us.

Jimmy was learned and eloquent. He used his bully pulpit as tour guide to hold the opposites. He spoke of the good the government has done in building much new housing. And he criticized it for its many failures. He took us to meet a woman I'll call Sheila, who lives in an old style hostel she shares with fifteen other families—a dark cramped space with one bathroom, whose toilet leaks, whose shower doesn't work. She calls the powers that be, frequently, to complain about the bathroom. They say they'll come. They never do. She shares her bedroom with the cooking stove for the entire place, her two children, and another family. This is a tiny room, maybe 7 by 8 feet. She's been there for ten years, waiting to get into new housing. She earns about $60 a month—not enough to buy her own place. I can still see her open, wide face. I saw determination in it, and a deep weariness. I hope she has gotten a new place to live. I wrote a poem about these experiences in Cape Town:

## Most Stony South African God

*In Suffering, and Nightmare,*
*I woke at last*

*to my own nature.*
—Frank Bidart

Table Mountain
Knife Edge Mountain

Altar Mountain where the Sacrifice is made
Most Stony South African God

*We see you*

You follow us all over Cape Town—
where Mandela spoke to the crowd—
*We see you*

At the Afro Cafe in the alley
red roses on orange and purple oil cloth
black girl entwined with her white lover
*We see you*

On Robben Island
where the writing on the wall reads:
"Happy Days are Here Again!"
William says he's still imprisoned—
can't get a job besides this—
being our tour guide in Maximum Security
*We see you*

At Langa, where Sheila and her sons
share six dark rooms, one stove, one broken toilet
with fifteen other families
*You have our number*

At the Langa Baptist church
held in the murmur of prayer
in Xhosa   in English
we call you JESUS   HALLELUJAH
*Forgive us for what we have done*
*Forgive us for what we have not*

Table  Mountain
Knife Edge Mountain
Altar where the Sacrifice is made; You Saw

WHAT THEY DID
TO STEPHEN BIKO
How the GIRL GOT BURNT

How the HEART SLUNK AWAY...
*What did we know?*
*What did we not know?*

O mountain
pull your cloud about you
gnash your teeth
*You've got our number*

Kitchen table mountain
sit us down with those
we'll never understand
Make betrayer meet betrayer
Make us eat our own stories

WHEN THE MOTHERS
LOOKED INTO THE FACES OF THEIR SONS'
MURDERERS, FOUND THE HUMAN
                          CORD—
                    *Where does it live?   Such Forgiveness?*

*What do we know?*
*What do we not know?*

Wise mountain
Dumb mountain
TOOTHLESS MOUNTAIN
GRINNING SKULL MOUNTAIN

Most Stony South African God
*You've got our number*
*Follow us home...*[18]

    *History is where the ends of the earth meet, where waters flow together, where the unpredictable happens.*
    Carly Vosters, a Jungian oriented therapist from Johannesburg—whom we had first met in Bulgaria—graciously offered to show us Cape Point—where the Atlantic and Indian Oceans meet—down the coast below Cape Town. The landscape is fierce and craggy—mountains jut

---

18  Lowinsky, first published in *Left Curve*.

out like the intricate hair designs I saw on African women—angles piercing the sky.

Carly spoke of the roughness of the landscape, which she loves. But, she told us, she misses the softer hues of her native Holland. She's been here for forty years, lived through the terrors and horrors of apartheid. She had to balance her political activism with her desire not to traumatize her children. We climbed up hill to see the end of the earth, where the Indian Ocean meets the Atlantic. The shore on the Indian side was floating on a ribbon of mist—as though about to take off into the sky. She invited me to come to Johannesburg, next year, to teach her Jungian group.

**The Shattering**

> *It is the duty of the living to heal their ancestors.*[19]

*History is a harrowing: it breaks us up like a harrow breaks the soil, so the seeds of the new can be planted.*

I knew that Jo'Burg was different from Cape Town. We had been warned about the crime, the security fences, the danger. That did not prepare us for the experience of actually being there. We stayed in Melville, a suburb of Jo'Burg, considered to be safer than the rest of the city. It was full of wonderful restaurants and bookstores; people of all races mixed easily; our B&B was elegant, yet it was protected by security guards and by metal fences and barbed wire. When we left its dramatic inner decor we had to unlock a metal door, turn around and lock it again. Then we'd walk a few steps to a metal fence that enclosed the compound, unlock the gate, turn around and lock it again. If we were going to breakfast, we'd cross the street, unlock yet another metal gate, turn around and lock it again. That was the drill…

On the second day of our visit, our hosts, Carly and Sem Vosters, picked us up in the evening. Dan and I had spent time with Carly in Bulgaria, on a bus tour of ancient sites, and become friends. We were meeting Sem for the first time. They are both Dutch, and had immi-

---

19  Malidoma Patrice Somé, *Of Water and the Spirit*, p. 10.

grated to South Africa as a young couple. Sem created a company which imports furniture. Carly is a Jungian oriented therapist who heads up the developing group. We were on our way to dinner with some other members of the group, at the Market Theatre restaurant. The Market Theatre was famous, during Apartheid, for anti-apartheid theater and desegregated audiences. We were in Sem and Carly's car. Sem was driving, Dan sitting beside him. I sat in the back seat by the window; Carly was next to me. It was dusk. We pulled up behind another car at a red light.

I saw a dark man in a hooded sweatshirt approaching. Was he going to ask for money, I wondered, or hijack the car? Suddenly the window was smashed and he was grabbing for my purse. Carly and I held onto that purse; to my surprise, we did not let him have it. Sem, a big man, reached back with a menacing look and the man slunk away into the shadows. My lap was filled with broken glass. We were missing a window in a questionable part of town. Sem drove through red lights—a common practice we were told.

*History is a shattering—of lives, of cultures…*

Glass kept shattering in my mind: The ghost of my father filled me with images of Kristallnacht—the night of shattered glass—when the Nazis broke the windows of Jewish businesses and homes and the denial of so many assimilated Jews was shattered. I was filled with images of the shattering of black South Africans lives, during Apartheid. Pumla Gobodo-Madikizela, writes of a shattering memory from her childhood in the township Langa:

> Big army trucks like huge monsters were roaming the streets, driving over walkways and…firing into the fleeing crowds. I was witnessing something I had never seen before: live shooting, blood and death. The image that remained in memory years later was that of a street covered in blood and bodies lined up like cattle in a slaughterhouse.[20]

---

20  Gobodo-Madikizela, "Memory and Trauma," in *Truth and Lies,* Jillian Edelstein, editor, p. 25.

Years later, when Gobodo-Madikizela served on the Truth and Reconciliation Commission, she was forced to understand that her memory was, factually, inaccurate. Only one person was killed that day in Langa. What she goes on to say is profound:

> When the safe world of a child is shattered by a violent invasion...the intensity of the moment presents itself as something that the world of a five-year-old cannot absorb. The child lacks the psychological capacity to contain the brutality before her eyes...Blood, bodies and death are the only meaningful words that capture in images what she cannot articulate in words.
>
> There is a parallel to be drawn here with adult experience. When we are confronted with unimaginable and unbelievable human brutality the effect is to rupture our senses...[21]

After the shattering in Jo'Burg, I began to understand my father—how shattered he had been by what had happened to his mother, his father, his sister, his people. That's why he needed always to be in rational control, why he was so fearful, so over-protective, why he could never trust life. Though ours was a small shattering, compared to the one that Gobodo-Madikizela described, Dan and I found ourselves much more open to others caught in the grip of collective trauma—we had landed in their world. I felt initiated into an aspect of the South African experience that I had tried to keep at bay: I could no longer look at all those metal gates, with electrified barbed wire above them, with my liberal Northern California eyes. I understood why people were living in fortresses, why so many people were leaving.

I learned that what had happened was called, a "smash and grab." It happens all the time. A spark plug is poked into a car window, causing it to shatter. I invited the smash and grabber into my psyche, asked him what this is all about. He said, *You people have so much. We have so little. After the end of Apartheid we thought we'd get what you have. It hasn't happened. If black presidents can't make it happen, we'll just smash and grab our way to what should be ours.*

---

21 Gobodo-Madikizela, "Memory and Trauma," in *Truth and Lies* p. 26.

The great South African novelist, J.M. Coetzee, writes of a black-on-white robbery as "Booty; war reparations; another incident in the great campaign of redistribution."[22] Pumla puts this into context:

> Black people are having to deal with the reality that political transformation has not fundamentally transformed their lives, while white people who benefited from apartheid have lost little or nothing…[23]

I sat with the members of the Developing Group in the cozy comfort of Carly's home, surrounded by metal fences and electrified barbed wire. I had been with them now for over a week in many settings. I found myself moved and impressed by them. Some came from families that had been in South Africa for generations. Others were the children of refugees from the Shoah—first generation, as am I. They were thoughtful, vulnerable, hospitable and generous. They taught me a great deal about their country. Most of them were profoundly conflicted—so relieved to be out of the shadow of Apartheid, proud of their country's revolution. Yet they felt imprisoned in their secure homes. It wasn't safe to take a walk, or to go out for a run. They seldom went out in the evening. They complained of governmental incompetence—whites with experience had been forced out. They suffered their own loss of power and status. But what was most unbearable was that their children had no future, could not find work in the new South Africa with its strong affirmative action policies.

At their request, I had presented my paper on the Shoah, spoken in the voice of my father's mother, who died in a concentration camp, told the story of my mother's parents, who left Germany in 1932. We had wrestled with Jung's *Answer to Job*. Jung says that Job is morally superior to the jealous, irritable God of the Jews. It is our human task to make Him conscious of his dark side.

How does that pertain to Africa, I wondered, hoping we could find our way into a less Eurocentric version of the problem of collective trauma and divinity. There was talk of the trauma they are experienc-

---

22  J.M. Coetzee, *Disgrace*, p. 176.
23  Gobodo-Madikizela, "Memory and Trauma," in *Truth and Lies,* p. 30.

ing. Many are Jews, caught in post-Shoah "phantom narratives," which, according to Jungian analyst Samuel Kimbles, are expressions of "a traumatized cultural unconscious."[24] They don't feel protected by the South African police. I heard, under the surface of their talk, a fear that their lives will be shattered by a wave of revenge against white South Africans. Nobody says this aloud. But the question arises, like a sudden gust of wind, forewarning a storm: "How did your grandparents know it was time to leave?"

Something is happening to the spirit of my father, something unfamiliar—a darkening—as though a shadow has passed over his luminous ghost. He's grieving—not something I knew him to do in life. He's grieving his parents, who did not get out of Europe in time, and his sister Ljuba, who stayed with their mother, hidden in a convent by nuns, until the Nazis found them and forced them to go to the concentration camp, Lag Westerbork. My grandmother Clara died there of cancer. Ljuba survived, to be transported to Bergen-Belsen. My father's spirit is even grieving his father, whom he bitterly judged in life, for running off with his Dutch girlfriend, abandoning his wife and daughter after the German invasion. The story I put together years after my father's death, is that his father was probably in a transport train on the way to Auschwitz in early 1943—six months before I was born—when the allies bombed the tracks. What an unbearable irony. My father did not live to chew on that one…

When my father lay dying of stomach cancer, I could not get him to reflect on his life's journey or on his losses. I had the intuition, watching that powerful being shrivel up into a fetal position in the hospital bed, that what was eating him was his undigested grief and guilt.

Even now, in his ghost form, I can't get him to stay with his grief for long, or to contemplate the impossible situation this group of white South Africans faces. He doesn't want to consider their dangerous options and unknowable fates. He wants to praise Mandela. He says, This is an entirely different story! Mandela is a great man, with a great affirming vision. It takes generations to bring such a vision into every

---

24  Kimbles, *Phantom Narratives*, p. 32.

day life. It's a difficult transition, and there will be many problems, but this is not Hitler's Germany!

I see the seduction of that leap—the avoidance of the terrible tension these people must live with every day. It is a spiritual problem—the difficulty of staying with the terrible, the unknown, the dangerous. It is my problem as well as my father's. But it would be disrespectful to the reality of what the group was facing, to jump to the positive, as it would be dangerous—prophesy fulfilling—to jump to the negative. I may not know in my lifetime whether Mandela's big soul was able to begin a transformative process, or whether it would turn out to be merely a light-filled moment, after which the forces of hatred and vengeance would take over. Perhaps it will be an entirely different story—one we cannot yet imagine, any more than my father could have imagined a Germany with more progressive social policies than those of his beloved America.

How could I hold this group, with respect for what they are facing?

## Maker of the Moon and Also of Trouble

*You can still change the world by dreaming the world,*
*you still have your tricks, old unteachable, untameable...*[25]

*History is an enchanter, a transformer, a weaver of new worlds.*

South African poetry was my vehicle. Poetry can hold so many opposites without falling into political or cultural stereotypes. We read poems by black South Africans. We read poems by white South Africans. We read poems translated from the aboriginal /Xan people, a few of whom, just as their own culture was being shattered, told their myths to Europeans. Mantis, a trickster, maker of the moon and also of trouble, was our guide:

---

25  Stephen Watson, "The Nature of /Kaggen," in *The Lava of This Land*, Denis Hirson, editor, 9.

## The Nature of /Kaggen

> /Kaggen, old trickster, magician, also called Mantis,
> maker of the moon, of the eland, and also of trouble,
> though you lie in the fire, your flesh now on fire,
> though you lie there writhing in the coals' red heat,
> your skin blistered, in tatters, your bones blackening fast
> (and how you deserved it, you scoundrel, always picking a fight!)–
>
> You can still change the world by dreaming the world,
> you still have your tricks, old unteachable, untameable,
> you could still make an eland from a piece of old shoe,
> old incorrigible, magician, old /Kaggen you slyboots...[26]

Poetry lives this side of magic, close to the realm of casting spells; its origins take us back to shamanic trance, to the oral tradition that tells a people's story. As the group read the mythic language, moving round the circle, each voice taking its turn, we were understanding the truth that shattering is a part of the human condition. I can count on my father's spirit to respond to the arts. He brightens, having found his own story in the poem, for he too was a survivor of the fire, he too was "an old incorrigible," he too changed the world by "dreaming the world." The ghosts of the /Xan, or Bushmen—ancestors of us all—joined us, reminding us how they had lived peacefully in Southern Africa for thousands of years, creating elegant rock paintings, hunting and gathering, initiating their young, until their world was shattered by other tribes, by agriculture, and by white men stealing their lands.

Poetry connects us to the web of voices which have been praying, invoking, telling and retelling, singing of love and suffering and death, transforming experience with sound, rhythm and image since the /Xan singer, since Enheduanna, since Homer, Sappho and the Psalmist.

The great Afrikaans poet Antjie Krog was a transporting voice during that afternoon circle reading in Johannesburg. We read her beautiful "letter-poem lullaby for Ntombizana Atoo." Written in Rwanda in 2000 it is a lullaby to a black baby. Here are some sections:

> I will come and claim you from bones and bullets and violence and aids

---

26 Watson, "The Nature of /Kaggen," in *The Lava of This Land*, pp. 8-9.

from muteness from stupidity from the corrupt faces of men
I'll gather you from millions of refugees
from hunger and thirst from the damp of cries
and the stink of tolerated grief
the desperate mangle of dreams…[27]

sh–sh
childest childling

child of mine
child of morrow
the veld lies loose in its skin of words

little girl, with wild plaits and cheeky slender neck
it is you, one day, making poems along the dusty road
      singing forward the way

yes! I see you[28]

The divine child is a black baby girl in a refugee camp in Rwanda; she will grow up to be a poet, "singing forward the way." The ghost of my father and I are in tears, for this poem expresses a love and a hope we've always shared. In the voices of these white South Africans, with their various phantom narratives, their fears and resentments, transported by Antjie Krog's lullaby, I heard their helpless, tender love for Africa.

We ended that afternoon with a poem, "River Robert," by the black South African Seitlihamo Motsapi. A poem whose magic held the opposites, it was written in 1994, the year Apartheid ended. The poet Tony Hoagland has written: "How strange it is that when I read a particular poem, which brings the world into focus for me, that I can feel my own self come into focus… The poem delivers me to a deeper, and more conscious state of being-in-the world."[29] That describes what this poem did for our circle. Here are parts of the poem:

  We bless the long rough road

---

27  Antjie Krog, "letter-poem lullaby for Ntombizana Atoo," *Body Bereft*, p. 59.
28  Krog, "letter-poem lullaby," *Body Bereft*, p. 61.
29  Tony Hoagland, *Real Sofistikashun*, pp. 171-2.

we bless the inscrutable darkness
where our names are rent into spirit
we bless the splinter & the air
we bless our lacerations & our deformities

we bless the belligerent strangers
who stay on in our throats
long after forgotten festivities

as we learn the painful lessons of love
as we learn to respect the night's sovereignty
& the slow stern wisdom of the desert
we bless the mysteries & the silence[30]

This lyrical poem—which blesses the things that have shattered the poet's world—puts me in mind of another shattering—the shattering of the vessels in the Kabbalistic legend. According to Isaac Luria—the 17th century Kabbalistic master—the first divine act was not emanation but withdrawal. It was called tsimtsum. Then came the shevirah—the shattering. The translator of Kabbalah, Daniel Matt writes:

"Most of the light returned to its infinite source, but the rest fell as sparks, along with the shards of the vessels. Eventually these shards became trapped in material existence. The human task is to liberate, or raise, these sparks to restore them to divinity"[31]

*History is luminous, filled with sparks of the divine, moments of illumination and redemption.*

I belong to the moment in 1945, when I was two, when my father invited the African-American tenor, Roland Hayes, to sing at Black Mountain College, and organized the first desegregated concert at a southern white school. I belong to the congregation in Langa, praying in Xhosa and English. I belong to the Jungians in Cape Town, so moved by Pumla Gobodo-Madikizela's description of the Truth and Reconciliation process. I belong to the group that gathered one afternoon in a comfortable home behind metal gates and bars in Jo'burg, and tried to

---

30  Seitlhamo Motsapi, "River Robert," in *The Lava of This Land*, editor Denis Hirson, p. 305.
31  Daniel C. Matt, *The Essential Kabbalah*, p. 15.

see into the future. I belong to my father's spirit, in gratitude and peace. Will it last? Has he changed? I'll let you know when I do.

# SECTION FOUR

# OLD MAGIC

## Chapter 7

## The Rabbi, the Goddess, and Jung[1]

*You cannot grasp these things unless you stumble over them.*[2]

## Spiritual Exile

*One who descends from the root of roots to the form of forms must walk in multiplicity.*[3]

How does a Jew to whom God never spoke in a synagogue, who has wandered the world and the paths of other religions seeking direct experience of the sacred, stumble upon it in her own tradition? How does a spiritual exile, whose life was transformed by the Goddess, get past her issues with the patriarchal God of the Jews?

With Jung's help…

This is the story of how Jung, or the Jungian worldview, helped me find my meandering way home to Judaism. As is my fashion, I weave in poetry, dreams, a journey, and a conversation with a ghost.

---

1 Lowinsky, first published in earlier form in *The Jung Journal,* Winter 2012, Volume 6, #1.
2 Matt, *The Essential Kabbalah,* p. 163.
3 Matt, *The Essential Kabbalah,* p.117.

I have always longed for myth, for mystery, for those moments when the world cracks open, when something uncanny, wild, awesome enters. I have glimpsed it in Hindu temples, in Catholic churches, in Pagan rituals, in poetry, everywhere but in the Jewish world I knew as a child. Here is a poem about my spiritual calling:

## what the high priestess says at the temple gates[4]

do not seek admission here
if your world holds together
      and everything knows its place in your house
          if the four walls have never fallen upon you
              or the living room furniture floated out

                  of a sunday afternoon
                      on the breath of some god

do not pester me with inquiries
or shine a light behind these veils
      if trees have never prophesied to you
          or deer danced among the white clay men
              in your back yard

do not disturb my meditations
      if your sky has never ripped open
          light cut you to pieces

            if your head's not been cra cked
              by the hooves
                of the bull god

            how can my mystery

                enter?

## The Ten Commandments of My Childhood

---

[4] Lowinsky, *crimes of the dreamer: poems*, p. 73.

> *There is a secular world and a holy world…In our limited perception we cannot reconcile the sacred and the secular, we cannot harmonize their contradictions.*[5]

It was a proud thing to be a Jew in my family of origin; it was also a difficult thing. We Jews had responsibilities. We had suffered as a people. We needed to be eternally vigilant, on the lookout for tyranny, oppression, discrimination—whether against us Jews or others. There were unspoken instructions for how to be a good Jew below the surface of dinner table conversations and in social gatherings in the very Jewish neighborhood in postwar Queens, New York, where we lived during the early 1950s. These are the commandments I heard:

I. Thou shalt vote Democratic.

II. Thou shalt take a stand against injustice and inhumanity.

III. Thou shalt believe in the innocence of Ethel and Julius Rosenberg.

IV. Thou shalt support unions and the ACLU.

V. Thou shalt love Paul Robeson, Roland Hayes, Marian Anderson and the Weavers.

VI. Thou shalt sing folk songs, spirituals, and union songs with gusto.

VII. Thou shalt know all the famous Jews in the culture and speak of them with pride, from Albert Einstein to Sammy Davis Jr.

VIII. Thou shalt love the state of Israel, but not forgive it its trespasses.

IX. Thou shalt know the stories of the Hebrew Bible, for thy father will tell them to you as "great literature."

X. Thou shalt never forget "what happened."

---

5 Matt, *The Essential Kabbalah*, p. 153.

I still live by most of these commandments. But notice, there is nothing about going to temple, synagogue or *shul,* nothing about God or the Torah. We were secular Jews and proud of it—my father's people before him and my mother's people before her. To be a Jew had little to do with religion. My mother insisted we join a temple, but that was about community. To be a Jew was about culture, ethics, values, history. To be a Jew—we learned from my father's dramatic rendering of bible stories at bedtime—was to argue with God and to fight with your brother, as did my brothers, as did Cain and Abel, Jacob and Esau, Joseph and his brothers. To be a Jew was never to forget our history.

My family's history was a terrible one. We were German Jews who had to flee Europe to escape the Nazis. Many did not make it, among them my father's parents. To be a Jew was to be in exile, to know persecution and oppression, to remember we were slaves in Egypt, to identify with black folk. There was no lack of religious feeling in my family, if, by religion, you mean those attitudes and practices that open one to the mysteries, the unfathomable, the divine. We did not enter those uncanny realms via Jewish rituals. Music was our chariot.

Music was my father's field. He was a professor of musicology—an authority on early music—Catholic Church music—human voices raised in praise to God. He was interested in how those voices wandered out the church doors and into the new consciousness of the Renaissance. Did my father ever ponder why he was drawn to religious music? Did he too long for the uncanny and the wild, the familiar world cracked open? I never heard him speak of what meaning his work held for him personally. Instead, he made a joke of it. He liked to tell a story about meeting a rabbi from Eastern Europe who asked him what he did for a living. He responded that he studied Catholic Church music. "Oy," said the rabbi, "what a Jew has to do to earn a living in America!"

In my early adolescence, my father was hired at UC Berkeley, and we moved to California. It was the late 1950s. There weren't very many Jews around town then. You couldn't get a decent bagel. At my mother's behest, we joined the reform synagogue. I struggled with my experience of the service, with its organ music and its suffocating air of rationality. My favorite place in the service was the "minute for silent meditation." I longed for the space to sink inward, to be receptive, to listen to what stirred in me. The rabbi, who was a kind man with good politics—he'd marched with Martin Luther King—raced past that minute in twenty seconds, as if the silence made him nervous or would agitate the congregation. I remember the bemused look on his face when I asked: "Couldn't we at least have a full minute of silent meditation?" I expressed my frustration with the rabbis of my youth in this poem:

## yom kippur visitation[6]

so you would rather
be left alone
on a wooden porch
naming the unnamable names
of the gods
as they appear to you
in a moon marked book

than sit among the congregation
of the ram's horn?

though you remember
being a girl who listened
to the rabbinical song on arch street
the rising and being
seated again
of jewish bodies
on metal fold up chairs
before they got permanent pews
the brown linoleum was speckled
like a goose egg

what if the one
who came in late
scraping chair legs
disrupting
the moment of silent
meditation

---

6  Lowinsky, *adagio & lamentation*, pp. 36-7.

was the thirteenth fairy
the snake in exile?

clearly the animal shriek
through ram's horn
was the only moment
god touched you
on the lips of a rabbi

was it then
that shriek owl
pounced on your beating heart
lifted you out of
the congregation
flew east
toward devil mountain

is this the same bird
    calling you now?

Lilith, in her shriek owl form, had lifted me out of the congregation and into the realm of the forbidden, because the only moment in the service that "God touched" me was that uncanny "animal shriek through ram's horn."

## It Was Our Period

*O Lady of mango breasts*
*of hips that reach for the moon…*

*Come back to me on screech owl wings*[7]

I was catapulted into a Jungian analysis in my late twenties. I had recently returned from India where the uncanny and the wild were everywhere. Back home I was adrift without the tumult of gods and goddesses, lost in a failing marriage, overwhelmed by three young children.

---

7 Lowinsky, *The Faust Woman Poems*, p. 21.

I had a bad dream. My three-year-old daughter's head was severed from her body.

My mother's voice said: "You'll never get her together again." A split between my head and my body was illuminated, a problem in the feminine was revealed. In the chariot of two long Jungian analyses, I found my way to the Goddess and began my long quarrel with the Hebrew God and the rabbis. I have written at length about these issues in my two prose books, *The Motherline* and *The Sister from Below* and in many poems. Here is a poem evoking those exuberant days in the 1970s, when so many of us were gripped by the reemergence of the "forbidden feminine."

## To My Long Ago Lady Delight[8]

Before you and the Serpent stopped being holy
Before Adam laid claim to cattle and hawk

Before you preferred exile with demons
to lying beneath him

Before Eve sank her teeth into God's own fruit
Before lust abandoned me

There was a time   my Lilith

when you were my own honey cave
My snake in the fervent grass

O Lady of mango breasts
of hips that reach for the moon

How long has it been since you sang
in my blood?

Come back to me on screech owl wings—Soar free
of your Red Sea spell—

---

8  Lowinsky, first published in *The Gathering*.

the time you've done
in wet dreams—

I long for you in my wild flower bed
Bring me your fire

As the territory of the "forbidden feminine" opened her sacred space to me, connecting me to my sexuality, my Motherline, my Sister from Below who is my muse, I found I had much to argue about with the Hebrew God. This God's prophets railed against the Goddess religions, against the divine feminine—the Asherath, the tree goddesses, the small clay figures of the sacred female form a woman could hold in her hand while she labored to give birth. As Leonard Shlain has argued in *The Alphabet Versus the Goddess*, the Jews were commanded to value abstract thought, in the form of "alphabet literacy" over the "graven image." He writes:

> Learning to think without resorting to images is indispensible to alphabet literacy. "Make no images" is a ban on right-brain pattern recognition. All who obey it will unconsciously begin to turn their backs on the art and imagery of the Great Mother and, reoriented a full 180 degrees, will instead seek protection and instruction from the written words of an All Powerful Father.[9]

I remember preparing to give a talk on the Goddess in a church. I was surprised to find, I was afraid—as though the God of the Patriarchy was going to get me for this. I had the following dream: I am about to go to the pulpit to give my talk when a rabbi in black robes races past me and begins speaking. He's stealing my talk—my time. And worse, his talk is dry, pedantic, boring. I realize I have to stand up to him—I have to make a scene—not something I like to do. I say, "Excuse me, Rabbi, this is *my* talk." I'm afraid he'll be angry at me, start yelling like my father did when crossed. But he just looks up, startled, and without a word, without a fight, walks away. It's as though he simply needed to be reminded that this was my time.

---

9  Leonard Shlain, *The Alphabet Versus the Goddess*, p. 83.

My Jungian chariot held me, allowed me to sink deep into my own nature, to steer the horses of my passions—the wild uncanny Goddess, poetry, and my continuing struggle with the God of the Jews and the rabbis. But the rabbis were changing shape. I dreamt of a rabbinical student with a scraggly beard and long fingernails. He was kept in a shed out back. He had no one to talk to. Perhaps he was autistic. Certainly he was being starved. When I engaged him in active imagination, he told me that he was a part of my Jewishness that needed attention. I began to understand that I needed to make peace with the Jewish God, to work things out with the rabbis.

I stumbled on a personal Yom Kippur ritual. I didn't feel drawn to the synagogue. I was pulled inward to dedicate this holiest day in the Jewish year to connecting to my inner life—tracking my dreams and poems, reading my journals. I've been doing this ritual now for many years and I find it deeply satisfying and orienting.

## Upside Down Tree

> *I am the one who planted this tree for all the world to delight in. With it I spanned the All, calling it All, for all depends on it, all emanates from it, all need it, all gaze upon it and await it.*[10]

I was given a gift of a dream. I am shown an image. It is an upside-down tree—whose branches touch the earth, whose roots are in the sky. The tree is filled with Hebrew letters. I did not recognize what it was, at the time, though the image stayed with me, tugged at me. At the time I was writing poetry and studying with the poet Diane di Prima. Diane is steeped in hermetic and occult traditions and considers them foundational to poetry. She taught the Qabalistic Tree of Life with its Sephirot, its Hebrew letters, its descriptions of the emanations of the divine in many forms. She works in the magical tradition, which spells Qabalah with a Q. Suddenly I realized what that dream was about—I had been shown the Tree of Life—the symbolic expression of Jewish mysticism. I had stumbled into the esoteric aspect of my own tradition, which I had

---

10  Matt, *The Essential Kabbalah*, p. 77.

thought lacked a mystical, contemplative side. The Kabbalah, whether spelled with a *K*, a *C*, or a *Q*, tugs at me. I was gripped by the ten Sephirot, the twenty-two paths, the four worlds. I meditated upon them and found that they weave together the realms of the visible and the invisible, body and soul, male and female, rabbi and Goddess, graven image and alphabet, the one and the many. The Kabbalah gave me ground to stand on, wisdom and mercy, severity and strength. It is a system of thought that speaks to the unfathomable in a way I can hold in my own life, that guides and encourages my spiritual imagination, gives me roots in the sky and branches on earth.

The early 20th century founder of the Society for Inner Light, Dion Fortune—an important figure in the Western magical tradition—wrote:

> The symbol of the Tree is to the Universal Mind what the dream is to the individual ego; it is a glyph synthesized from subconsciousness to represent the hidden forces…
>
> The Qabalistic Tree might be likened to a dream arising from the subconsciousness of God and dramatizing the subconscious context of Deity.[11]

## In the Garden of Pomegranates

> *Nothing is devoid of its divinity. Everything is within it; it is within everything and outside of everything. There is nothing but it.*[12]

Suddenly, the Kabbalah was everywhere. I stumbled upon it in Jung's writings. In his lovely essay on "The Philosophical Tree," Jung explained the upside-down tree, the *arbor inversa* as an image of the primordial man—Adam Kadmon—according to the Kabbalah.[13]

In that great cauldron of alchemy and the wisdom traditions, *Mysterium Coniunctionis,* Jung delighted me with liberal doses of Kabbal-

---

11  Dion Fortune, *The Mystical Qabalah*, p. 16.
12  Matt, *The Essential Kabbalah*, p. 24.
13  Jung, "The Philosophical Tree," *CW* 13, ¶ 410.

istic imagery. He goes on at great length about the sexual nature of the Sephirot:

> Yesod signifies the genital region of the Original Man, whose head is Kether. Malkuth...is the underlying feminine principle...The Cabala develops an elaborate hierosgamos fantasy... [about] the union of the soul with the Sefiroth of light and darkness, "for the desire (and here he is quoting the Zohar) of the upper world for the God-fearing man is as the loving desire of a man for his wife..."[14]

I began to understand the vision Jung had after his heart attack when he was hovering between life and death. In *Memories, Dreams, Reflections*, he describes being in the "Garden of Pomegranates" while the mystic wedding of Tifereth with Malkuth (the Shekinah) is taking place.[15]

Daniel Matt's little treasure book, *The Essential Kabbalah*, provides an amplification:

> In Kabbalah Shekinah becomes a full fledged She:...the feminine half of God. Shekinah is "the secret of the possible," receiving the emanation from above and engendering the varieties of life below. The union of Shekinah and Tif'eret constitutes the focus of religious life...Human marriage symbolizes and actualizes divine marriage.[16]

I knew this landscape. I had explored it with pleasure in the erotic images of Hinduism, in the "forbidden goddess religions," in poetry. This is the realm of sacred sexuality—considered an abomination by the Jewish prophets. Jung has no problem with it. In fact, it brings him back to life. He writes: "Sexuality does not exclude spirituality; nor spirituality sexuality, for in God all opposites are abolished."[17]

So the sexual and sacred feminine has a dwelling place in Judaism! I can be a Jew, a Jungian, and a Goddess worshipper, all at the same time?

---

14  Jung, "The Components of the Coniunctio," *CW* 14, ¶18.
15  Jung, *MDR*, p. 294.
16  Matt, *The Essential Kabbalah*, p. 9.
17  Jung, "Adam and Eve" *CW* 14, ¶ 634.

Who knew? My unconscious responded to this news with a dream of an ecstatic Chassidic rabbi, singing and dancing at a wedding. He threw me up in the air like a bride.

It was about that time that Sophia showed up in a dream and followed me into my morning meditations. She was beautiful—a light-skinned black woman. She created a glowing bridge for me between the Goddess realms and Judaism. She is Wisdom in Proverbs. She is the Shekinah. According to Philo, God creates the world by means of Sophia.[18] According to Jung, she is an "independent being who exists side by side with God."[19] According to Jeffrey Raff, she is the Tree of Life, also the light of the divine.[20] Perhaps she is the dark Shulamite, that "Priestess of Ishtar,"[21] of whom Jung writes in *Mysterium Coniunctionis,* who longs to "become like Noah's dove, which, with the olive leaf in its beak, announced the end of the flood…and God's reconciliation with the children of men."[22]

Perhaps she has appeared to announce my reconciliation with the God of the Jews. She led me to a strange synchronicity. My late mother-in-law, a devout left-wing atheist, took pride in her lineage, which goes back to the famous 16th century Rabbi Joseph Karo. In my readings, I stumbled onto a myth about this Rabbi Karo—his spirit guide was the Shekinah herself.[23] She consulted with him, as Sophia consults with me. The Rabbi, the Goddess, Jung, and my secular mother-in-law cohabit in my psyche, exchanging stories!

## Black Fire Written on White Fire

> *Twenty-two elemental letters. God engraved them, carved them, weighed them, permuted them, and transposed them form-*

---

18 Caitlin Matthews, *Sophia*, p. 97.
19 Jung, "Answer to Job," *CW* 11, ¶ 619.
20 Raff, *The Wedding of Sophia*, pp. 54-5.
21 Jung, "Adam and Eve," *CW* 14 ¶ 646.
22 Jung, *CW* 14 ¶ 625.
23 Matthews, *Sophia*, p. 118.

*ing with them everything formed and everything destined to be formed.*[24]

It must be She, the Shekinah, who is behind what happens next. In September 2004, I find myself in Gerona, Spain. My husband Dan and I have come here because it was a center of Jewish life and Kabbalistic thought before the expulsion of the Jews. Gershom Scholem, referring to Moses De Leon, the author of the *Zohar*, writes:

> He has drawn freely upon the writings published by the school of Kabbalists whose center was the little Catalan town of Gerona and who between the years 1230 and 1260 did more than any other contemporary group to unify and consolidate what was pregnant and living in the Kabbalism of Spain.[25]

We are staying in a small hotel at the edge of the old Jewish quarter. The narrow streets of the Jewish section have in recent times been excavated. One can see the layers of life that have covered over Gerona's Jewish history. Chaplin, who has written a memoir about the mysteries of Gerona, describes the city well:

> Bells rang across this forest of stone every fifteen minutes, day and night. The cobbled alleys and crumbling stairways, the deep arches leading to unexpected courtyards, were all stone, medieval or pre-Roman…The stone made the town echo… It was said that the stones had a magnetism…I've heard it's to do with the ley lines. At certain points across the earth the energy builds up and creates a pull, a pulse, and in these places unusual and mystical things can happen.[26]

I certainly feel that pull and pulse in Gerona. I sit on the tiny balcony of our hotel room and try to focus on each Sephirot, despite the sounds of passing people, cars, motorcycles, water being poured, conversations in Spanish, Catalan, Italian, English, despite the bells of the Cathedral. I

---

24 Matt, *The Essential Kabbalah*, p. 102.
25 Gershom Scholem, *Major Trends in Jewish Mysticism*, p. 173.
26 Patrice Chaplin, *City of Secrets*, pp. 5-6.

imagine the rabbis meditating—making contact with God amidst donkey piss and roosters crowing and children running about and bed pans being emptied.

In the evocative Museum of the History of the Jews, I learn that there were Jews in Catalonia since the 1st century AD. Jews owned houses, had a synagogue. During Spain's Golden Age, Jews, Muslims, and Christians coexisted, mostly in peace, for centuries. But by the end of the 14th century, restrictive actions were in place against Jews. They couldn't have shops, couldn't touch certain foods. They had to wear a sign—the red circle indicating that they were Jews—prominently on their clothing. I walk among the gravestones, which are displayed in the museum, and I am moved by the translations of Hebrew epitaphs.

> Grave of Dolça, the honorable…keep her memory alive in the world to come, she who went to her eternal resting place in the month of Av of the year 5000.
>
> He took pleasure…in the Lord. He was pious with the poor and kept away from Evil. God fearing he passed away…Clean of faults. His name was R. Reuben, son of R. Hanina. May his memory live on forever.
>
> He went to his eternal place of rest in the month of Av in the year 5103 of the computation of the Creation; may his soul be bound up in the light of the living ones.
>
> House of Jacob, walk…towards the light…

In my wanderings in the old Jewish section of Gerona, I happen into the Nahmanides Institute of Jewish Studies. I learn that Moses ben Nahman (nicknamed Ramban by the Jews, called Nahmanides in the Greek fashion of the day) was a leading Kabbalist in the 13th century in Gerona. He was of the generation before the *Zohar* was written down and one of those who influenced its writer, Moses de Leon. Ramban "was convinced that there is another level of meaning in the Torah: the secret one…"[27] which was understood only by those who know the Kab-

---

27 Moshe Idel and Mortimer Ostrow, *Jewish Mystical Leaders and Leadership in the 13th Century*, p. 39.

balah. He did not believe in the written transmission of these mysteries.[28] Ramban did, however, write a famous commentary on the Torah, in which he said that the Torah was "originally written with black fire on white fire."[29] That beautiful image clings to me, mystifies me.

Rabbi David Cooper, a leader of the Jewish Renewal movement, compares the more rational thought of Maimonides to the mysticism of Ramban:

> In response to Maimonides' viewpoint that miracles are used by God to reveal Itself to the masses, Nahmanides suggested that a level of reality supercedes nature, and in this higher reality, the miraculous is commonplace. Nahmanides said that a miracle is not a singular event in contrast to the flow of nature, but rather that miracles are an ongoing process. The only reason we think that a miracle is opposed to the ordinary flow of nature is because we do not have a broad enough scope of this other dimension.[30]

But there is another side to this Ramban. Gershom Scholem comments on how rare it is to find a great Kabbalist who has also contributed to the mainstream rabbinical tradition.[31] Ramban was such a rabbi. He is famous for his participation in the "Disputation of Barcelona" in 1263. King James I invited Ramban to participate in a religious debate. His opponent in this spectator sport was a zealous Dominican friar, Pablo Christiani, who wanted to hasten the conversion of the Spanish Jews, "by convincing his opponent that the Messiah had indeed come in the person of Jesus and that the Jews' most Jewish of texts [the Talmud] proved it.[32] The historian, Jane S. Gerber writes:

> Despite…the fervent arguments of Christiani…Nahmanides was so impressive that the Franciscans asked that the debates be discontinued, and the crowd in attendance grew unruly.

---

28  Idel and Ostrow, *Jewish Mystical Leaders and Leadership in the 13th Century*, p. 40.
29  Scholem, *On the Kabbalah and Its Symbolism*, p. 38.
30  Cooper, *God is a Verb*, pp. 131-2.
31  Scholem, *Major Trends in Jewish Mysticism*, p. 125.
32  Gerber, *The Jews of Spain*, p. 101.

James I ended the disputation, but he supposedly remarked to Nahmanides, "Never have I seen anyone who was in the wrong argue so well as you have."[33]

Ramban was accused of blasphemy and forced into exile. A man in his sixties, he had to leave his family and walk alone to Palestine.

I am filled with the presence of this rabbi. Later, in my readings, I will stumble upon a reference to a Jewish myth in which the "spirit of a departed sage…fuses with the soul of a living person." This spirit is called an *ibbur*, in contrast to the malevolent spirit known as a *dybbuk*.[34]

I find myself talking to him: Ramban, I walk the Roman walls of your city and your light walks with me. I walk the narrow streets of the Call de Jueu and the light you received from Moses at Sinai walks with me. You speak in my heart. This light, you tell me, is not of memory, not of the history of our people, not the word remembered and written down. This light is now. Are you angry with us Ramban, that pale reflections of your light are written into books?

Ramban, there was much thunder in the night, and bolts of lightning. That, and the church bells and the sounds of trucks. You would not recognize such a commotion. Sun returns to a city washed clean by rain, like a woman emerging from the mikvah you say. Your bright spirit is standing on the spiral stair, waiting for me, you've been waiting…

I wonder why it is you who have come to guide me, you who are at once a mystic and a learned Rabbi of the tradition. You say it is because I need to learn your teaching, that "Everything that is done in the mundane sphere is magically reflected in the upper region…"[35] You say I listen too much to my fears. I need to open all my senses to the Shekinah. You say I need to contemplate the mystery of "black fire written on white fire,"[36]—the tension between the oral tradition and the radiance, between manifest wisdom and the transcendent. Because you want me to understand that the Goddess is alive in you, that The Sister

---

33 Gerber, *The Jews of Spain*, p. 108.
34 Schwartz, *The Tree of Souls*, p. 333.
35 Scholem, *Major Trends in Jewish Mysticism*, p. 233.
36 Scholem, *On the Kabbalah and Its Symbolism*, p. 38.

from Below is your familiar, you recite a stanza of your mystical hymn about the birth of the soul:

> *He radiated light to bring her forth,*
> *In hidden well-springs, right and left.*
> *The soul descended the ladder of heaven,*
> *From the primeval pool of Siloam to the garden of the King.*[37]

You say our souls stand in eternity, they are forever, we spend our lives finding our way back to them, for we are in exile from our beginnings. You say the light is now, here in this place where we meet. It is not about memory, not about history, not the word remembered and written down, but now. Despite that you want me to write you down, to make you a poem, to sing you a song, because you know I need to. Here it is:

## God's Singing Tree: In Two Voices

> *When the forms are destroyed, the root is not destroyed.*[38]

### 1. Ramban

> I walk the Roman walls of your city    and the light
> you received from long before Moses
> walks with me    through the narrow streets
> of the Call de Jueu    you speak    This light
> you tell me    is not of memory    not    of history    not
> the word    remembered and written down
>                                                 This light is now
> and you are in it    here on a tiny balcony
> in the early evening    where church bells ring
> each quarter hour    not far from the synagogue
> no longer a synagogue    where they have made a library
> in your name    (you who believed in the oral transmission

---

37  Scholem, *Major Trends in Jewish Mysticism*, p. 240.
38  Matt, *The Essential Kaballah*, p. 117.

                              you who argued against writing it down)

Holy holy holy is the word you were given
and your soul is bound up
                              in the light of the living ones

## 2. Ramban speaks

> *You don't know it 'til you lose it    the radiance*
> *of a life   You are shaped by your times like bread*
> *is braided for the Sabbath    and so it seems*
>
> *it will always be like this    children playing peacefully*
> *in the garden   the chant of the shema   intertwined with*
> *the bells of the cathedral   Who can say why*
>
> *it changes   There is a shift   a rip   a disputation*
> *is required   my knowledge is dangerous    and suddenly*
> *I am an old man   in exile   in Palestine*
>                                 *generations before*
>                                                *the expulsion*
>
> *We thought it was the end of time    but time went on*
> *other countries   other ways   other tongues    where*
> *did the children of my children go    and the disciples*
>
>                              *of my disciples?*

## 3. Dream Teaching

Ramban
does it trouble you
that I write down
what I hear you say?   Such pale reflections
of the mystery you teach    I need the written
word    for I have wandered and lost
my orientation   I have forgotten the names
of my ancestors and that there is a secret
in our stories   forgive me   Ramban    if I stumble about
in the holy light   forgive me if I stutter

> *You will stumble for that is the way*

*You will stutter   for how else does one say
a mystery?   You will wrestle with my words
in notebooks   on your strange new writing
machine        Do not let yourself be stopped
by some law you imagine   some tradition
you don't think you understand   My daughter*

*I have waited for you on the shining stair*

*I was mute and ragged in your dream from years ago
kept in the back shed  with the chickens and goats
some yeshiva bocher you did not know was in you*
                                    *kept me alive*

*or you confused me with that rabbi in black robes
who suffocated breath     drained light
stole magic    from the Torah
The congregation rose
sat down again   creaked chairs
shuffled feet      You believed
that sacred music belonged
to the Catholics    that ecstasy belonged
to the Sufis    that the breath of fire belonged
to the Hindus      that the tree goddess
who entered you when you were a child
and filled you with her green joy
was an abomination in the eyes
of the fathers    No wonder you fled
No wonder it took you most of a life
time wandering from Orissa to Thrace
to Catalonia to recognize me
that dancing rabbi  in your dream
who threw you into the air*
                                    *as a bride*

## 4. God's Singing Tree

Ramban
you are old magic with goddess eyes
you are warm fire in the dark of the cave
you gather me back to the breath of that mother

in the long long line of my great grandmothers
who picked up her baby   her sack of food
and walked out of Catalonia in 1492

The vessels shattered    there was contraction
there was exile          You tell me
this is the nature of creation

        They who listen will hear
        They who open their eyes will see
        There is a tree   it grows from the feet
        of Abraham and Sara   its leaves catch the light
        on this balcony where I sit with you

        *Remember    my daughter*
        *wherever you are    the poem is*
        *black fire written    on white fire*
                              God's singing tree

    The flow of this long story has carried us over six decades—from the child in Queens hearing the secular commandments of her people, to the frustrated adolescent longing for spiritual experience, to the young mother with a bad dream about the severed head of her baby girl, to the young woman who began finding her Self in the chariot of Jungian analysis, who was freed to claim her true nature through the Goddess and her muse, *The Sister from Below*. From the perspective of maturity, this strikes me as the kind of ongoing natural process Ramban recognized as a miracle. It seems miraculous to me that the Rabbi has been so profoundly transformed in my psyche, from one who "suffocated breath" and "stole magic" into one who is "old magic with goddess eyes." It feels like magic to me that the Rabbi, the Goddess, Jung, and my dear secular mother-in-law—may she rest in peace—can enjoy each other's company and exchange stories in my imagination. Like the dark Shulamite, in Jung's description toward the end of *Mysterium Coniunctionis*, I have "wandered among the mazes of…psychic transformation" and come "upon a secret happiness…a secret love…a hidden springtime, when the green seed sprouts from the barren earth, holding out the promise of future harvests."[39]

---

[39] Jung, "Adam and Eve," *CW* 14, ¶ 623.

# Chapter 8

# Drunk with Fire
## How *The Red Book* Transformed My Jung[1]

*Support me for I stagger, drunk with fire. I climbed down through the centuries and plunged into the sun far at the bottom. And I rose up drunk from the sun…*[2]

## A Distant Fire

*I am weary, my soul, my wandering has lasted too long, my search for myself outside of myself…*[3]

There has been a breach between Jung and me. How could that happen? I had no idea who I was until I met Jung, nor had I had a decent conversation with my soul. Jungian analysis showed me my way into the world, and into my inner life—it opened the door to the poet I'd left behind in my childhood. But when I encountered Jung's suspicious attitude toward artists—so like a Swiss burgher—the poet in me was offended.

---

1 Lowinsky, first published in an earlier form in *Marked by Fire*.
2 Jung, *The Red Book*, p. 272.
3 Jung, *The Red Book*, p. 233.

Enter, *The Red Book*. When I sat down with that enormous tome on my lap and leafed through its gloriously illuminated pages, its visionary poetry, its astounding paintings and mandalas, my heart opened to my illustrious ancestor—all was forgiven. I felt vindicated. Jung, as I'd always suspected, was a closeted poet.

What is this *Red Book*? During a difficult time in his life, after his break with Freud, Jung was deluged with powerful images and visions. He wrote them down and painted them. He created a strange and beautiful book—bound in red leather—to hold them. It looks like a medieval illuminated manuscript. *The Red Book* was not published, even after his death, because of concerns that its wild, prophetic tone would cause people to dismiss Jung as a mystic or a madman. When it finally came out in 2009, it surprised the Jungian world by creating a media sensation and selling out its first printing. But, I am getting ahead of my story. Before I tell you how Jung and I reconciled, how we became drinking buddies by the primordial fire, let me give you some history of our relationship.

I first met Jung in my late twenties, when I found *Man and His Symbols* on a remainder table. I didn't know what I was buying into. There he was, in the frontispiece photo, the wise professor at his desk with his pipe and his books—mysterious images glowing behind him. Jung's essay, "Approaching the Unconscious," was introduced by an unforgettable photo: doorways within doorways grew smaller and darker, pulling the eye from the opening door frame decorated with Egyptian figures deep into the unknown of the tomb of Ramses III.

At the time, I was lost in my life, a single mother of three, full of terrors and complexes, with no sense of self. In a Jungian analysis, I felt seen and heard for the first time in my life. I learned to listen to the unconscious, to the charged magnetism of dreams, and to heed the rich vein of inspiration that arises mysteriously from within to guide a life. My Jungian path was revealed; my fire was lit. Jung has been a teacher, a wise man, a guide to a deeply lived life, ever since. But my experience of Jung's fire has been hermetic—from an unseen place in the center of the earth.

Years ago, when I began consulting with Joe Henderson—a founder of the San Francisco Institute who had been in analysis with Jung—I dreamt that in the middle of Joe's consulting room, there was a round stove, which Joe called a "funda." I knew that its heat came from the center of the earth. *Funda*—foundational, at the bottom, at the base. *Funda—fundus*—a word for womb. Heat from the womb of the earth is a good image for the fire from the depths that my Jungian training tended. But it was a distant, impersonal fire. And Jung was a distant figure, sitting at his desk full of alchemical and magical texts.

He showed up in a dream as a trickster, waggling his eyebrows like Groucho Marx, handing Joe Henderson some pieces of silver to hand on to me. It wasn't Jung himself, but his wife Emma, who, in a dream, helped me dress for an upcoming meeting with the Certifying Committee in which I hoped to become a Jungian analyst. She gave me a blouse embroidered with a large tree of life. It looked like the oak tree I'd known as a girl. That oak had given me her lap to sit in: she had given me her strength, her calm, her roots, her far-reaching green hands. In her embrace, I'd daydream and write poetry. With the help of Emma Jung and that oak, I was certified.

Despite his distance, Jung and his followers—my analysts, consultants, teachers, colleagues—gave me the tools I needed to follow my own charged path. I found my way back to that oak, and to the poet I'd been as a girl. This is when Jung and I began having problems. Now that I was both an analyst and a poet I was upset by his distrust of artists. There is a passage in his memoir, *Memories, Dreams, Reflections,* in which Jung expresses this distrust. He is writing down his "fantasies"—that is, working on *The Red Book*—and asks himself:

> "What am I really doing? Certainly this has nothing to do with science. But then what is it?" Whereupon a voice within me said, "It is art." I was astonished. It had never entered my head that what I was writing had any connection with art. Then I thought, "Perhaps my unconscious is forming a personality that is not me, but which is insisting on coming through to expression."[4]

Having understood that he had an inner figure whom he called the *anima*, Jung went on to accuse her, and artists, of treachery, even of psychopathology:

---

4  Jung, *MDR*, p. 185.

> What the anima said seemed to me full of a deep cunning. If I had taken these fantasies of the unconscious as art, they would have carried no more conviction than visual perceptions, as if I were watching a movie. I would have felt no moral obligation toward them. The anima might then have easily seduced me into believing that I was a misunderstood artist, and that my so-called artistic nature gave me the right to neglect reality.[5]

Neglect reality? No moral obligation? Was Jung buying into that tired old stereotype of the artist as a big child, an *enfant terrible*? The artists I know use their creative work to attend to what's real and what's ethical—that's how they get below the surface to touch the essence of things. Poetry and prose are how I express my moral obligation to the dead, to the suffering, to the neglected in myself and in the world.

In most of his writings, Jung keeps a studied distance from the direct experience of the charged path, from the pandemonium of the irrational. If he's drunk with fire, he's holding his liquor well. Though I can understand, rationally, why Jung would need to be a "suit" rather than a "creative," a scientist rather than a poet—why he would need to look relatively sober in his *Collected Works*—I have felt wounded by his dismissive attitude toward the artist, hurt that this powerful ancestor misunderstood the very development in me that his psychology had helped me claim. There was a breach between Jung and me—we tended different fires, honored different lineages, though I never tired of pointing out to my inner Jung, in teaching and in writing, that his ancestor and mine—Goethe—was a poet.

## Soul's Fire

> *The spirit of the depths forced me to speak to my soul, to call upon her as a living and self-existing being. I had to become aware that I had lost my soul…*[6]

With the publication of *The Red Book*, my Jung has been transformed. He is "outed" as a poet and a painter. He writes directly out of his vulnerability,

---

5 Jung, *MDR*, p. 187.
6 Jung, *The Red Book*, p. 232.

working out his relationship with his soul in the depths of the mythopoetic imagination, just as I do. In *The Red Book* Jung reclaims his soul—or rather she reclaims him. She appears to him and becomes his guide. She is an inner figure with a mind of her own. This honoring of the voice from within, which Jung would later call *active imagination*, is one of his greatest gifts to me. Instead of ignoring or dismissing voices that speak from within, Jung taught me to listen and to engage in dialogue with them. When "The Sister from Below"[7] began speaking to me, telling me she was my muse, my soul, my writing life took off.

Recently, I dreamt that my friend Gilda Frantz and I were driving north to see Jung. I told her I was excited to see him again, since I had known him as a child. *The Red Book* speaks to the child in me. I grew up in a German-speaking household. Though nowadays my German is rusty and childlike, the sound and feel of the language tugs at a primal place. I feel a resonance with the book's beginning phrase: "*Der Weg des Kommenden*"—the way of what is to come. This is the magnetic pull of what wants to be realized, what yearns to be born. It was the creative task of *The Red Book*—to open Jung to his depths, to redeem his soul and his gods.

Jung's elegant calligraphy and illuminations invoke another aspect of my childhood. My father was a musicologist, a historian of the early Renaissance. His soul spoke to him in illuminated manuscripts. I was drawn to them as well. But I was a first-generation kid trying to look American. None of my friends knew an illuminated manuscript from a comic book. When I was first writing poetry in my twenties, I actually had the idea of illuminating my poems. It was one of those passionate ideas that devoured me. I took a calligraphy class. I made an illuminated version of a poem as a gift to my mother in Chicago. I asked a friend who was traveling there to carry it to her. He left it on the plane—it disappeared into some black hole—as did my plans for further illuminations. It is mysterious and moving to me that Jung did this thing I had longed to do.

When he implores, "Support me for I stagger drunk with fire," I feel a tug and am deeply moved. Why is this? They are wildly poetic words—in the Dionysian mode. They take me down to that primal level of religious feeling—worship of the sun, our source. I know the states he describes. To

---

7 Lowinsky, *The Sister from Below: When the Muse Gets Her Way.*

be drunk with fire tells it all—the creative ecstasy—at once wildly enlivening and demonic—fire as Dionysus, fire as Shiva, fire as Pele. Certainly being a poet can mean being drunk with the sun from the bottom of time. One finds oneself climbing "down through the centuries"[8] pursuing a word, an image, a phrase of goat song.

It has been essential for me to write directly out of the experience of being in other realities, rather than describing such states from a safe distance. In *The Red Book*, Jung contains his intense and overwhelming experiences by writing them down, by painting them. I recognize that urge. I have shelves and shelves of journals in which I've worked to contain my own fire, to follow inner figures, to work with poems and with dreams, to dive below the surface of the times to what is moving in the depths. And I always feel better, more grounded, more real to myself after I do.

## Primordial Fire

> *An old secret fire burns between us. The words uttered at the fire are ambiguous and deep and show life the right way.*
>
> *[We] will respect the holy fire again, as well as the shades sitting at the hearth, and the words that encircle the flames.*[9]

Enter, the Sister from Below. She's got an idea:

*Why don't you take your own advice? Do an active imagination with Jung, now that you feel this warm glow of kinships libido for him? Imagine you two are sitting by the primordial fire, as he puts it:*

This makes me nervous. Jung is the master of active imagination. Is it hubris to invoke him? But I have learned to listen to the Sister. So I sit down with my notebook. Jung, I discover, is reluctant. He is not at all sure he wants to engage in this exercise. Why not? I ask.

*Because I am a fantasy of yours.*

I know that. That's why I referred to "my Jung" in my subtitle. You're like Izdubar, in your own *Red Book* story—the god from the East you can

---

8  Jung, *The Red Book*, p. 272.
9  Jung, *The Red Book*, p. 280.

save from Western rationality only by calling him a fantasy. You carry him around in your pocket, like an egg.

*Yes, but he embodied Eastern wisdom and philosophy. I was a mere mortal, a man of my own time, far from your fantasy Jung.*

I understand that. But you are an ancestor. "Take pains to waken the dead."[10] Those are your words. I don't want you to be dead in me. Just as I've had long conversations and written many poems about my personal dead, and the collective dead, I think it is important for me to have a living relationship with you.

Jung, still looking like Groucho Marx, still hanging on to his trickster nature, waggles his eyebrows at me and says:

*OK. I'll talk to you, as long as you never forget I'm a fantasy. What are we going to talk about?*

How about poetry and art? How my poetry is the way soul speaks to me, helps me contain what might otherwise burn me up. I think the poetic nature of your writing in *The Red Book* enables you to contain immensities, unbearable intensities.

*Well, you need to understand it's never been about art for me. Writing, painting, making* The Red Book *was all about trying to grasp the unfathomable, the divine.*

Poetry is that for me, too. I too reach for the unfathomable in words. I do see, however, that there is a difference between your practice and mine. What you made is, I think, very beautiful. But I gather that beauty was not your objective. It is mine. For me it is a form of spiritual devotion to revise and revise. Not so much with my head, but with my body, all my senses. I love what you say about words as symbol:

> The symbol is the word ... that rises out of the depths of the self as a word of power and great need and places itself unexpectedly on the tongue. . . . If one accepts the symbol, it is as if a door opens leading into a new room whose existence one previously did not know.[11]

---

10   Jung, *The Red Book*, p. 244.
11   Jung, *The Red Book*, p. 311.

This describes my experience of feeling my way for just the right word/symbol when working on a poem. It must carry that depth charge that opens new rooms. Here's a poem for you. It has fire in it, and a dream.

## I asked for a dream

    and because you coughed in the night

    I remembered
    the fire
    painted by the woman
    who had been through it all—
                    her testimony to the ones who burned—

    she mixed her own
    colors
    red with just the right yellow

        for the blaze
                  green
    with a touch of purple
                  for foliage
                  violet for the pretty horses
                            our flesh sacrifice  O

                            the leaping flames to god

    you turned in bed and groaned about what
                      you wouldn't remember—

    the woman who painted fire in my dream
                      held it up for me
                          to see through[12]

My phrase, "her testimony to the ones who burned," refers to what happened to my people in the Shoah; it refers to my dead, to whom I feel a deep obligation. Like you, I'm haunted, and I feel a kinship with you, sitting by the primal fire, when I read your words:

---

12 Lowinsky, *crimes of the dreamer*, p. 3.

But the spirits of those who die before their time will live, for the sake of our present incompleteness, in dark hordes in the rafters of our houses and besiege our ears with urgent laments, until we grant them redemption …[13]

The Jung of my fantasy responds:

*The woman who paints fire in your dream, paints it so you can see through it, not be devoured by it. It's easy to be devoured by the dead.*

I know that. I was being devoured until I stumbled into my first Jungian analysis and learned to listen to my dreams. But as you say, one can be "held fast by the dead," they can keep one from one's work, because they demand atonement. Much of my writing is in the service of that atonement. Here's a poem for the dead:

## Lullaby of Lineage

If only I knew how to ride a melody
backwards in time

I'd visit my father in Stuttgart, a hundred years ago
He's four

He's wandered into the music room
with that dreamy look I remember

His mother stands in the doorway
watching a ray of light

touch his face. She's enchanted
by her son—how green his eyes

how delicate his fingers and his bones
That melody in minor mode, he picks out

on the keys, is that the lullaby
she used to sing to him? If I could be

---

13 Jung, *The Red Book*, p. 297.

a particle of light, one of the dust motes
floating about this family of Russian Jews

recently escaped from Pale and pogrom
If I could linger in this moment, taste its sweetness

before the First War, before the Second War
before Rachel weeps for her children again

Surely I could find my way to you
O daughter of the daughter of my daughter's son

Once I have slipped out of this flesh
into the dance of particles

A hundred years from now
Surely I could be a dust mote in a ray of light

touching you—your hands on your belly
in that gesture I'll remember from when I had a body

woman with child
Surely you will feel me—your agitated ancestor

I'll want to know you have survived
floods, fires, famine, wanderings to higher ground

I'll wish I had a human voice to sing to you
that old lullaby, played by my father

on the piano—in minor mode
when he was four.[14]

*I see, says Jung, you are haunted and you intend to haunt. Your poem sounds like my writing about the Eleusinian Mysteries, which celebrate Demeter and Kore, mother and daughter.*

---

14  Lowinsky, first published in *Soundings East*.

Yes. That was a great gift you gave me, when you wrote "every woman extends backwards into her mother and forwards into her daughter.[15] You gave me the image of an individual woman as a bridge between the ancestors and future generations. That was the kernel of my first book *The Motherline*,[16] and led me to my passion for the goddess.

*But I notice you used your Motherline bridge to take you back to your father as a child—a very tender image of him.*

Thanks for noticing. So many issues that I have been wrestling with for a lifetime come together in that poem. It's a working through of my relationship with a difficult father. When I imagine him as a four-year-old, enchanting his mother with his musical gift, and put them in their historical context, Motherline and Fatherline are joined. Paradoxically, honoring my father and his mother in this way releases me from bondage to the patriarchy: giving him his due frees me to follow my goddess. For She who was reviled, forgotten, forbidden, has been redeemed, brought back into consciousness in me and in the culture at large. You saw this coming in your enthusiasm about the Assumption of Mary. I've seen the goddess catch fire in the imagination of my generation. Here's a poem about that:

### A Brief History of Mothers and Daughters

> We were the daughters of girdled mothers, Jell-O mold
> mothers, mothers schooled in the uses of Lipton's Dried
> Onion Soup, mothers who dusted every other morning,
> taught their daughters how
> to iron a man's long-sleeved shirt: first the collar
> then the shoulder yoke, poking the hot metal nose
> between white buttons. We were the hungry daughters
> of mothers long severed
> from the moon in their thighs, long severed
> from what had called them
> when they were seventeen. We promised ourselves
> never to be our mothers....

---

15 Jung, "The Psychological Aspects of the Kore," in Jung and Kerenyi, *Essays on a Science of Mythology*, p. 162.
16 Lowinsky, *The Motherline*.

We were the daughters of Moon Tide, of Life Lust,
of what insisted on coming through us. We smoked it.
We drank it. We ingested its Magic
Mushrooms. We saw molecules dance in a leaf, in a stone.
We were daughters
of First People, of rivers, of trees. We belonged
to each other. We belonged to the earth. Mystery
called us by name....

We leapt out of marriages, invoked Forbidden
Goddesses—
the ones the prophets railed about—you know who I
mean: The Whore of Babylon, the Golden Serpent,
the Temple Dancer. It was She
who moved in our bodies, She who tasted the fruit, She
who was exiled from the Garden— She
whom our mothers never dared
to imagine—sat alone, chanting sultry verses
by the Red Sea...
Everything was possible.
We could leap over the moon
We could chant
      write
            paint
                dance
                    make love like warm rain
                    make love like wild surf

It was Our Period.[17]

*You were certainly drunk with that fire!* Jung is laughing at me.

Oh, I was. That fire is quieter now, but still illuminates my worlds.

We sit for a while, in silence, watching the primordial fire, my fantasy, Jung and I.

## Catastrophic Fires

---

17 Lowinsky, first published in *The Spoon River Poetry Review*.

> *I find epidemics, natural catastrophes sunken ships, razed cities, frightful feral savagery, famines, human meanness, and fear, whole mountains of fear.*[18]

There is a sudden commotion in the air, a rustling of skirts and shawls, and here she is, my Sister from Below, come from the bottom of beyond to join us at the primordial fire.

*You might have invited me,* she says. *This is my kind of fire.*

You don't usually require an invitation, I say. You just show up. Why now?

*I'm here to ask your man Jung a question on your behalf.*

Jung looks interested: *Are you this woman's soul?*

*I am. But I want to ask you about your soul—her terrible prophesy of fire—not the fire of ecstasy, not the fire of the hearth or this holy fire we sit around—but the fire of catastrophe. Your soul spoke to you and said:*

> I see the surface of the earth and smoke sweeps over it—a sea of fire rolls in from the north, it is setting the towns and villages on fire, plunging over the mountains, breaking through the valleys, burning the forests—people are going mad...[19]

The Sister says: *I too see terrible fires. I too prophesy catastrophic times. You were a mortal, how did you tolerate that fire?*

I jump in before Jung can speak: in my life I have lurched from fear of the fire I came from—the Shoah—to fear of fire as atom bomb, as Agent Orange, as suicide bomber, as global warming. There's always something new to fear. How did you stand it?

Jung sighs: *With great difficulty. The fire threatened to engulf me. It took painting mandalas. It took major efforts on the part of my soul, Izdubar, Philemon, and all the others. My soul told me I had to sacrifice fear—a difficult thing to do. One has to keep sacrificing it everyday, sometimes with every breath, like meditation, like yoga.*

---

18 Jung, *The Red Book*, p. 305.
19 Jung, *The Red Book*, p. 346.

*You listened to your soul, to your muse,* says the Sister from Below, *and made a work of art to hold yourself together. Your soul knew that writing and painting are magic.*

I join in: Poems are magic. They are prayers, invocations, spells. I love what you say about magic:

> Everything that works magically is incomprehensible, and the incomprehensible often works magically... The magical... opens spaces that have no doors and leads one out into the open where there is no exit...
>
> Magic is a way of living. If one has done one's best to steer the chariot, and one then notices that a greater other is actually steering it, then magical operation takes place.[20]

My Jung is laughing at me again: *I can see what you're up to. You're trying to convince me that I'm an artist after all, because* The Red Book *saved me, as your writing saves you. But it saved me to become who I was—not an artist but an empirical scientist of soul. I stopped using words like* magic *so people would take me seriously. But you and I can agree that magic exists, that it is a way of living, of working, that it inhabits language.*

My Sister from Below speaks to me now: *You don't need Jung to call himself an artist. You just need to remember that his soul and I are sisters from the bottom of time. You know from me, you know from him that you need to surrender in order to feel a "greater other" steering your work, taking you some place you didn't know you needed to go. When you started this paper, you didn't know you'd be sitting by the holy fire with your fantasy Jung and me, now did you? Thanks to me, thanks to him, you've "squandered"[21] decades on this opus of wandering inner worlds, writing poems that steer you into a new way of seeing. Jung has said: "This life is the way, the long sought after way to the unfathomable which we call divine."[22] Poems are your way. I think of your poem "Sisters of My Time" in which you invoke your generation's revelation of "that Old Black Magic," testify to the catastrophic times you're aging*

---

20  Jung, *The Red Book*, p. 314.
21  Jung, *The Red Book*, p. 330.
22  Jung, *The Red Book*, p. 232.

in, and gather the harvest of your life to leave as emergency rations for the daughters of your daughters. This, thanks to your Jung, is your legacy.

## Sisters of My Time

What became of our fierce flowering? Don't you remember
how that Old Black Magic revealed Herself to us—gave us the fever
the crazy nerve to burn bras, leave husbands, grow animal hair?
We knew Her belly laugh, Her circle dance
Her multiple orgasms—It was Our Period.

What became of us—Our Period long gone—stuck
in traffic jams, eaten by Facebook—gone stale
amidst the unwept unsayable? Some of us burst
our vessels. Some of us descended into cellars—
ghosts among the apricot preserves.

Meanwhile our bones thin, our skin loosens, our hands
can't handle a mason jar. And our Red Queen, what of her?
Her rain forests are bleeding out. Her corn won't tassel,
Her cattle are dying of thirst, Her Ivory Billed Woodpecker—
that God Almighty Bird—has not been heard for a generation.

Our Lady of Ripening's gone on a rampage—hot flashes
in the heartland, fire in the forest, flood
in the bayou, weeping
ice caps. Our grandchildren starve
for Her belly laugh, Her circle dance.

Now is the time, Sisters, to gather
what spells we know, what seeds we've cultivated
what Oracle speaks in our dreams, for the root cellars
of memory, the mason jars of prayer—emergency rations—
for the daughters of the daughters of our daughters

long after that Old Black Magic

                        has spirited us away…[23]

---

23  Lowinsky, first published in *The Book of Now*, ed. Leah Shelleda.

# SECTION FIVE

# GRANDMOTHER SPIDER'S SONG

## Chapter 9

## Earth Angel and the Tohu Bohu[1]

*To the Woman in the Earth*
*Who is my first and ever beloved*
*Whose smiles and rages and storms and weepings…*
*are my life, my terror, my thought, my wild joy…*[2]

### Where Have All the Weather Gods Gone?

*Earth does not belong to us; we belong to the earth.*[3]

There was a time, not so long ago, when weather was the business of the gods. Zeus—the king of terrible weather—threw thunderbolts, ravaged the earth with storms and hurricanes. So did Indra, Thor, Celtic Cally Berry, Slavic Perun and Yuruban Shango. Poseidon created storms at sea, as did Japanese Susanowo. Aeolus made the winds blow, as did Sumerian Enlil and Pawnee Hotoru. Even the God of the Hebrews began as a Storm God with a terrible temper. Ask Noah. Ask Job.

---

1 Lowinsky, first published in an earlier form in *Psychological Perspectives*, Volume 57, #2, 2015.
2 Gunn Allen, *The Sacred Hoop*, epigraph.
3 Chief Seattle, http://thinkexist.com/quotes/chief_seattle/

Divinity revealed itself in the form of bad weather, and we humans were awestruck and full of dread. So we prayed, made sacrifices, did rain dances to change the minds of the gods—to change the weather. Bad weather creates chaos, and chaos is our terror—threatening everyone and everything we love. The Greeks saw Chaos as the god of the air, of the gap between heaven and earth, the god who throws us into the great unknown. Yet Chaos, the Tohu Bohu, as it is written in Genesis, is a necessary state before Creation—a "condition prior to cosmos."[4] Artists and poets would agree.

But the gods died and weather lost its high stakes status. In recent times, unless we are farmers or sailors, talk about the weather is considered "small talk," shallow—a way of avoiding deeper conversation. That is, until a series of brutal winters began scaring us out of our delusions of safety and control. Chaotic events became the stuff of every day. In early 2014, a "Polar Vortex" brought the climate of the North Pole to the American Midwest and South. Meanwhile, at the North Pole, glaciers kept melting. In February 2015 winter storm Octavia thrashed the South and East, finishing the punishment begun by Winter Storm Neptune which had its fierce way with the Northeast and Midwest. (Maybe the gods are alive after all). Flights were delayed and the Federal Government was shut down. In March of the same year Kentucky was hammered by blizzards, motorists were stranded on Highway 65 on the way to Louisville, and Boston had recorded more snowfall—108.6 inches—than had ever fallen in weather memory. I hear this on the news.

It was 10 degrees below zero. The pipes were frozen. You had to melt snow to make tea. This was in an e-mail from my friend Richard Messer in Ohio.

There's been no rain in California. The warm weather is sweet, seductive, makes us feel guilty and uneasy. The governor stands in a meadow in the High Sierra, where there are many reporters but no snow, and proclaims, Year IV of the Deepest Drought in 1200 years. He orders us to cut back water consumption by 25%. I wonder, where is the other 75% coming from? There is no snowpack.

---

4 Joseph Henderson in *An Encyclopedia of Archetypal Symbolism*, ed. Beverly Moon, p. 12.

Farmers who dig wells are going so deep into the earth that they are pumping water from the Pleistocene—water from the time of the Wooly Mammoth, 18,000 years ago—"pumping like there's no tomorrow," says an exasperated expert on the radio.

The National Oceanic and Atmospheric Administration declares an "unusual mortality event" among baby sea lions on the California coast. They are beaching themselves in unprecedented numbers—starving and sick. The warming oceans may be their problem, driving their food into deeper waters. I learn this online.

Pope Francis takes on the prophetic function of a spiritual leader. Speaking of capitalism he says, "In this system, which tends to devour everything which stands in the way of increased profits, whatever is fragile, like the environment, is defenseless before the interests of a deified market, which becomes the only rule." I read this in the December 2013 *New Yorker*, the one on whose cover the Pope is a friendly snow angel.[5] He writes of the shameful truth that the god we really worship is the market.

The Vatican announces plans to host a major climate change conference in April 2015. And the word, at this writing, is that Pope Francis is soon to release an encyclical on the moral issues of environmental degradation. This news comes online.

## The Devil and Grandmother Spider

> *There is a spirit that pervades everything, that is capable of powerful song and radiant movement, and that moves in and out of mind. The colors of this spirit are multitudinous, a glowing, pulsing rainbow. Old Spider Woman is one name of this quintessential spirit.*[6]

Enter, an enormous spider, bigger than I am. A shady character throws Her at me. I am terrified. This happens in a dream. Awake, I remember

---

5  James Carroll, "Who Am I to Judge?" in *The New Yorker*, Dec. 23, 2013, p. 88.
6  Paula Gunn Allen, *The Sacred Hoop*, p. 13.

Grandmother Spider, who spins the web of the world. The world-wide-web tells many of Her stories. The Cherokee say that the people lived in darkness until Grandmother Spider stole the sun.

In another story, She keeps the sky from drifting away from the earth by spinning them back together. It is Grandmother Spider who saves us from chaos.[7] In Hopi legend, She is the Creator Goddess. She spins the thread which connects East and West, North and South. With Her breath She creates sun, moon and stars. She and the Sun dream up Earth and all Her creatures by singing the First Song. She attaches Her thread to all creatures, all people and tells us to call on her if we need Her. Perhaps the world hangs by this thread.

Jung says something like that: "…the world hangs on a thin thread, and that thread is the psyche of man."[8] But reading about Grandmother Spider on the world-wide-web does not do justice to the dream, which was visceral and shocking. It clings to me like a sticky spider web and stuns me with mortality. I have to bow to Grandmother Spider, a great goddess from millions of years before humans. What does She want from me? Should I be talking to Her? Is She some sort of animal ally? I can see Her clearly—eight hairy legs, eight baleful eyes. Looks like She'd sooner bite me than speak. I turn to the shady character who threw Her at me in the dream. "Will she speak to me?"

*Not a chance*, says he. *She's not your ally, not your friend. She goes back eons before humans. She doesn't need you, nor does She believe Earth needs you. But people need Her. First people knew how to honor Her. You don't.*

"Why do you throw her at me?" I ask.

*I'm throwing the Book of Life at you and your kind. You have sinned against Grandmother Spider.*

"Who are you to talk to me that way?"

*You know me well. I come to you in many forms. You know me as the Tohu Bohu—instigator of chaos. You know me as Satan, who bets with God that Job, once deprived of his good fortune, will lose his moral compass. You know me as Mephistopheles, the Devil in Goethe's Faust. "I am part of the force that always tries to do evil and always does good…part of the dark-*

---

7  http://www.mikelockett.com/popstory.php?id=100
8  *C.G. Jung Speaking*, pp. 303-4.

ness that gives birth to light."⁹ I'm the trickster who liberates Faust from his melancholia, his stuck life in the gray walls of academia and then proceeds to get him into all kinds of trouble. You know me as coyote, who shows up as you walk in the hills and meanders into your poems. The spider I throw at you is a form of the Earth Spirit whom Faust summons with a magic spell. Faust feels powerful, inflated—his magic has worked. The Spirit says: "I am birth and the grave, an eternal ocean, a changeful weaving, a glowing life. And thus I work at the humming loom of time, and fashion the earth, God's living garment." The Earth Spirit proceeds to mock Faust, stamps on his self-regard, calls him "a worm wriggling away in terror."[10]

I know that kind of terror. Since I was a very young child. I've been watching the thread on which the world hangs, fearing it will break. As the child of refugees from the Nazis, I knew my family's survival hung on a thin thread of fate and determination. I came to consciousness in the era of nuclear terror—the madness we knew as "Mutually Assured Destruction." In my early adulthood our collective fears shifted to environmental catastrophes—burning rivers, a great hole in the ozone, oil spills, clear-cutting of rainforests, decimation of species. In the 1960s, environmental legislation cleaned up the air and the rivers, revived many species. But the political climate has changed and we are in a time of dangerous denial. It is hard to know how to proceed with the weather gone crazy and Grandmother Spider in a nasty mood. She's a trapper. What if we get stuck in her web and she pierces us, stuns and devours us?

Maybe that's already happened. We think we are masters of the universe, but Grandmother Spider has us in the grip of Her eight feet, stunned, paralyzed. I know why that shady character thinks we have sinned against Her. We have lost our essential connection to the natural world, to the "anima mundi." She comes to remind us of Her power. What are we supposed to do now?

---

9   Goethe, *Faust*, Barker Fairley Translation, p. 21.
10  Goethe, *Faust*, Barker Fairley Translation, p. 10.

## The World Before Highway 24

> ...the shaman makes contact with the purveyors of life and health...by propelling his awareness...into the depths of a landscape at once both sensuous and psychological, the living dream that we share with the soaring hawk, the spider, and the stone silently sprouting lichens...[11]

When I feel troubled, unsure how to proceed, I go to my books for wisdom. Jung has much to say about these matters:

> Man feels himself isolated in the cosmos because he is no longer involved in nature...Thunder is no longer the voice of an angry god, nor is lightening his avenging missile. No river contains a spirit, no tree is the life principle of a man, no snake the embodiment of wisdom, no mountain cave the home of a great demon...[12]

Jung's lament fills me with a familiar sadness. It is the sadness I feel when I contemplate first people, those ancient ones who walked the land I live on now, who knew it as sacred. Driving home from work one night, I have a vision during a lunar eclipse. It becomes a poem:

## Where the Buffalo Roam

> A sky herd of buffalo stampedes the moon—I see it
> driving on 24. The radio says
>
> the shadow of earth will steal the moon—
> our only moon—but I tell you
>
> It is a thundering ghost herd of buffalo
> that shoulders the moon out of her sky
>
> The moon disappears in her deerskin dress
> The ghost dancers stamp and beat their drums

---

11   David Abram, *The Spell of the Sensuous*, p. 8.
12   Jung, *Man and His Symbols*, p. 95.

They chant the world before Highway 24
when earth was home to the buffalo

when the people followed the dance
of the sun, when they knew each story of rock

each spirit of mountain, of tree
what flowered, what died, what came back

as the moon came back in her deerskin dress—
our only moon—

in her radiant light
I look at the sky over 24

but the buffalo are gone…[13]

David Abram—a philosopher and a magician—has made a profound impact on the environmental movement with his dazzling book, *The Spell of the Sensuous*. He writes of being initiated into the natural world and its spirits. He had to spend the night in a cave in Bali to wait out a storm. He describes the wall of water that poured over the mouth of the cave as he watched spiders weaving "overlapping webs…radiating out at different rhythms from myriad centers…I sat stunned and mesmerized before this ever complexifying expanse of living patterns upon patterns…I had the distinct impression that I was watching the universe being born, galaxy upon galaxy…"[14] Abram continues:

> I have never, since that time, been able to encounter a spider without feeling a great strangeness and awe…They were *my* introduction to the spirits, to the magic afoot in the land. It was from them that I first learned of the intelligence that lurks in non human nature.[15]

This story fills me with hope. It reminds me of a book I loved when I was a girl—*Green Mansions*. I wanted to be Rima, who lived in the

---

13 Lowinsky, first published in *The Book of Now*, ed. Leah Shelleda.
14 Abram, *Spell of the Sensuous*, p. 16.
15 Abram, *Spell of the Sensuous*, p. 17.

jungles of Guyana and knew the language of the animals and the birds. But I'm no Rima. Neither am I a David Abram. Most of us aren't. What hope is there for those of us who don't spend the night in caves or swing through the jungle from trees? How do we open ourselves to Grandmother Spider's magic? How do we remember that Earth is our Mother, our Ground of Being, our Tree of life, Our Rock of Ages, our Beloved—the source of all our blessings—our only Home? Jung writes:

> …we have increasingly divided our consciousness from the deeper instinctive strata of the human psyche…Fortunately, we have not lost these basic instinctual strata; they remain part of the unconscious, even though they may express themselves only in the form of dream images. [16]

Thank the gods for dreams. That enormous spider holds the secret that connects us to our deepest wisdom—below the human strata, below the mammalian strata, down to the insect level. She spins Her web from Jung to the ghost herd of buffalo, to Abram, to Rima, to me, as I begin to see what that shady character in my dream is up to. The Devil is a fallen angel, an angel who brings the taboo back into consciousness. He is hell bent on breaking through the walls of our narrow, scientifically oriented worldview. Science is a great human development but, as both Jung and Abram lament, it often de-spiritualizes nature. Abram writes:

> The world in which we find ourselves before we set out to calculate and measure it is not an inert or mechanical object but a living field, an open and dynamic landscape, subject to its own moods and metamorphoses.[17]

## Great Song

*Her feet are listening*
*Song of the earth*
*holds her now*[18]

---

16  Jung, *Man and His Symbols*, 52.
17  Abram, *Spell of the Sensuous*, 30.
18  Lowinsky, "Her Next Life" in *The Little House on Stilts Remembers*, 5.

In the pilgrimage of my reading, I come across these words from Jung: "Every country or people has its own angel, just as the earth has a soul."[19] Suddenly, my heart is filled with singing. I'm hearing "Earth Angel," that teenage love song from my youth: *Earth Angel, will you be mine? My darling dear, I love you all the time. I'm just a fool, a fool in love with you.*"[20]

I remember that Grandmother Spider and the Sun sang the world into being. Though I can't fathom why she chose this song, I realize Grandmother Spider has trapped me, devoured my consciousness. She has tied me to Her by heartstrings, by music, by the long ago longings of adolescence. I see whom I must address. She comes to me in the midst of this terrifying winter, shape-shifting from enormous spider to Earth Spirit to a winged being who tells me She's my Earth Angel, and needs to have a talk with me.

*It's about time you noticed me. I am the ground on which you stand, the source of your life and your food. You build your great cities on me. When I quake, towers fall. Why do you look down on me, try to control me, devalue me, see me as dumb, dead, mute, inert, to be used and abused at your will? There was a time when you listened to me, knew I was born of the song sung by Grandmother Spider, honored me with dances and with sacrifices, When you were a child your parents placed you on me. You learned to sit up, to crawl, to walk on me. You loved me then, felt my breezes, listened to my birds sing. You were in paradise. You wrote a poem about it.*

## My Eden

(Black Mountain College, 1943-47)

Garden of the sun dappled baby I was
and the towheaded toddler, I can see me now
on the wooded path, beloved of the morning

and the night, drunk on mother's milk

---

19  Jung, *Letters II*, 432.
20  Written by Jesse Belvin and Curtis Williams. Recorded by the Penguins in 1956.

and daddy's lullabies, cradled in the rapture
of the mountains, captivated by the fiery flash

of a Cardinal in flight, seer of the light
in willows, and in the waters of Lake Eden
enchanted by the song of the Carolina Wren

transported into sleep on wings of Bach and Schubert
enfolded as I was in this Black Mountain tribe
of music makers, paint stirrers, pot throwers, leapers in the air…

Outside the gates—news of the war
Smoke rose, bombs fell
Inside the gates—faculty fights

for or against, communism, twelve tone music, short shorts
on young women. In the basement of the cottage named
Black Dwarf, a Moccasin frightened my mother. But I

lucky baby, took my first steps
between your apple and your wild
rhododendron, greedy for the names of your every living thing

Early I lost you. Lately I've found you
again. Sweet spot, source
of the singing in my heart, and my communion
                                                    with the mountains…[21]

    I wish I still felt that sweet communion with you, with the mountains, with every living thing. Instead I feel disoriented, lost. The fabric of the seasons is ripped. The sky is drifting away from the earth. Chaos threatens—the gap between Heaven and Earth, the gap the Hopi say you mended. That's what we need now, your weaving, not some banal love song from the 50s which turns you into an angel.
    *Why not come as a teenage love song? It worked. It got your attention. You got past your paralysis and couldn't get my song out of your head. Why not come as an angel? Angels are messengers. Every god needs an angel to translate between god talk and human talk. That's a form of weaving. My*

---

21  Lowinsky, first published in *New Millennium Writings*.

*job is to speak for Earth, to remind you that She is a great goddess. She speaks in forest, in meadow, in river and mountain, in meadow and in lagoon. She speaks in weather. You've been ignoring Her for ages. I'm here to be Her translator. Everyone has an Earth Angel—the place where you were born, took your first step, the place that shaped your earliest memories, the place you describe in your poem—just as everyone is connected to Grandmother Spider if only they'd notice the thread.*

*I have known you forever, way before you were born. I told you all the mysteries while you were curled up in your mother's belly—the secrets of life and of death, who you are meant to become. Then I placed my forefinger on your upper lip to silence you. You forgot most everything I said, though sometime shards come back to you, in dreams, in visions, in voices that speak through you and demand to be made into poems. It is my voice that speaks in your poem, "Lailah Wants A Word.*

## Lailah Wants a Word

> *Lailah, the Angel of Conception…watches over the unborn child.*
> —Jewish Legend

You were not born for traffic
Not released into day for hustle

and drive. I did not send you past moonstone
past glow worm, to ignore the light. I did not touch

the soft spot on your crown, nor seal
my blessing on your upper lip, to be a slave

to acquisition. I sent you into the company
of frogs. I sent you to commune with willows

with oaks. Pay attention—
the frogs have stopped wooing

the oaks been sold down river

Grandmother Spider   Brother Rabbit

are losing their worlds. You have ears —
Hear them.  You have a heart—feel them

You have two lungs—breathe
I give you the wind

in the grasses. I give you the sight
of Coyote.  She's meandering up

the mountain.  Follow her.  Perhaps she will throw
your shoe at the moon.  Perhaps the moon

will fill your shoe with shimmer—
Sail it back down to you—Then

will you remember
                      Me?[22]

*As you can tell,* Earth Angel says, *I'm angry. I speak for Earth and She is angry. She speaks in Super Storms—Hurricane Sandy, Typhoon Haiyan. She speaks in the Polar Vortex and the California drought. How much more explicit does She need to be?*

*And you, in your mad dash from here to there, are severed from Earth. You don't feel Her with the soles of your feet, don't see Her as sun glitters through the liquid amber trees, don't hear Her as the crows scold you, don't smell Her in the morning dew or taste Her ripe tomatoes or dig in Her with naked hands to plant roots. You forget to listen to the river god; you are blind to the spirit of the tree; deaf to the voice of the mountain and the lagoon. You read books. You don't read your Mother Earth.*

Sometimes books bring me back to you. I read Jung's words about every country having an angel and you appear singing "Earth Angel." But I still don't get what a song about a teenage romance has to do with climate change and rising seas. Seems a far cry from the Great Song Grandmother Spider sang with the sun.

---

[22] Lowinsky, first published in *The Book of Now*, ed. Leah Shelleda.

Earth Angel responds: *Human love is a form of my mystery—my web of life. Even when people seem to have forgotten creation's Great Song they sing bits of it. As another song says, "Birds do it, bees do it, even educated fleas do it. Let's do it, let's fall in love."*[23] *You used to be in love with me. You used to worship me. You used to sing my geography as song lines in the dreamtime. You used to speak to my rocks, do rituals in my caves, dance your story and mine. Your body, your walking pace, used to fit into me naturally. You knew me by walking me—sang me as you walked me—read me as you sang me.*

## Car Brain

> *The core of the mind is the ecological unconscious. For ecopsychology, repression of the ecological unconscious is the deepest root of collusive madness in industrial society. Open access to the ecological unconscious is the path to sanity.*[24]

Earth Angel continues:

*A man is walking across the world. In the New York Times Sunday Review, he writes that he is trying to put himself "in a Pleistocene state of mind"… but "cars keep roaring into my awareness. They are without a doubt the defining artifacts of our civilization. They have reshaped our minds…"*[25] *He describes his difficulty getting directions from people who only know the earth as drivers, whose "frame of reference is rectilinear and limited to narrow ribbons…axle-wide, that rocket blindly across the land." Such people, he says, are "spatially crippled."*[26] *He calls this condition "car brain." You suffer from it, caged as you are in a metal machine that severs you from me.*

I respond: But wait a minute, we humans are tool-making creatures. It's part of *our* nature.

---

23  "Let's Do It." Written by Cole Porter in 1928.
24  Theodore Roszak, *The Voice of the Earth*, p. 320.
25  Salopek, "A Stroll Around the World," *New York Times Sunday Review*, Nov. 24, 2013, p. 1.
26  Salopek, "A Stroll Around the World," *New York Times Sunday Review*, Nov. 24, 2013, p. 1. 6.

*The problem is not with your tools, but that you forget you are a part of nature, forget that without me, you're nowhere, forget you live on Earth. As Abram points out, though you say "the sun rises," and "the sun sets," whether you are a farmer or a physicist,[27] you are split off, dissociated from that real subjective experience, for, as we all know, the earth moves around the sun. You damage me and don't understand you are damaging yourself. You pave over my fertile soil, clear cut my habitat, extinguish innumerable species of my creatures, remove my mountain tops, slaughter my whales and my elephants. Your greed and your hubris sever your erotic connection to me. You forget I'm alive. You've turned me from your loving whisperer of mysteries—your spirit guide—into a terrible angel bearing dread tidings—melting glaciers, super storms, warming oceans. I don't think you're listening. I'm pulling out my green hair!*

I respond: You need to understand, we humans get paralyzed by grief, by fear, by guilt. We'd rather deny the realities of your terrible tidings than face what may become of us in flood, in fire, in drought, in famine—what might become of our children, our grandchildren. Honestly, I don't know how to respond to your warnings, your fury. I'm not a naturalist, not an environmental activist. My life is lived in houses, in cars, in rooms. I hear you in my inner life. Only sometimes do I visit with you out of doors.

## Wild as Rima

> *And you,*
>
> *old ecstatic*
> *of trees,*
> *have you forgotten*
>
> *Green Mansions—that slip*
> *of a girl who first lit*
> *the green fire?*[28]

---

27  Abram, *Spell of the Sensuous*, p. 40.
28  Lowinsky, "Wild Girl of Pleasant Hill," in *The Little House on Stilts Remembers*, p. 19.

Earth Angel responds: *I've come to you in rooms, in houses. I've come to you again and again, in your inner life. Remember, when you were a child, I was your "Lady Tree." You drew me with brown, green and blue crayons at the kitchen table—a rooted figure with breasts and arms that were branches raised to the sky. Your father laughed at your drawing, found Her silly. You learned to keep your sacred experiences to yourself.*

*I came to you when the children were grown and you moved into a house at the top of a ridge. I taught you my dance with the sun, from summer to winter and back. I gave you the Great Horned One, who hooted at night on your roof—who caught you in His terrible gaze. I gave you poems.*

That's all true. It was your inspiration that gave me back my early love of poetry in a house that worshipped your beauty. What an irony that people who love the natural world build their houses in those dangerous borderlands where fire or flood have eminent domain. Though I loved that house I always felt it encroached on sacred ground. I wrote a poem about that.

## Where Coyote Brush Roams

*Well they'd made up their minds to be everywhere because why not.*
—W.S. Merwin

We were high on the sky when we lived on that ridge    high
on the red tailed hawk    high
on the long green rumps of the hills going yellow
while the sun did its dance from winter to summer and back    high
on our ridge after work while the fog flowed over
the darkening hills we poured red wine on the earth    high
on escape from the city's exhaust    high
on the song of the frogs in the pond
some man had made
                      never mind

that the pines and the cottonwood trees
knew they didn't belong up there    never mind
that electrical towers asserted their rights
that coyote brush said the land was its own
that the ridge wanted fire and we did not
we weed whacked    cleared    cut down those pines    never mind

that we heard their cries in the night
though they never belonged up there     never mind
that the frogs went away one day and so did we…

The ancient ones who walked these lands
who made their arrows from coyote brush
knew not to make one's home on a ridge
for a ridge will insist on fire

> home is in a valley
> by a river among cottonwoods

We live in the valley now where once there was a river
             where frogs once sang in spring

                                        never mind[29]

It's a terrible dilemma we're in. I have no idea what to do.

*You're missing the obvious fact that is right under your nose. Your tool is poetry. That's what you do. Because I'm your Earth Angel, your Earth Spirit, a friendlier incarnation of your Grandmother Spider, I have given you the tools of your own nature, that essence of you that creates your thread and weaves your early muse, Rima, into your suburban setting with its malls and freeways, its gas stations and former farms. You called that poem, "Wild Girl of Pleasant Hill."*

## Wild Girl of Pleasant Hill

Once this was somebody's
grandparents' farm—sweet
as Rebecca of Sunnybrook—
do you remember?  How she skipped
among meadows with wildflowers,
til she was thrown
like a sheep
to the ground,
shorn of her corn, her hay.

---

29  Lowinsky, first published in *Fourth River*.

But she's still here, that girl.
You'll see her playing in the fountains
near Rotten Robbie's Gasoline
or herding her geese by the Chinese
All-You-Can-Eat Buffet,
while cars zoom past on 680
in sight of the mountain.

You'd think she'd be dead by now—
after all the concrete that's been poured.
But that girl is
wild as Rima—
talks to the willows, to the birches,
laughs aloud at the ducks
who have commandeered
the community
swimming pool.

And you,
old ecstatic
of trees,
have you forgotten
Green Mansions—that slip
of a girl who first lit
the green fire?

Talk to her—
your wild friend from beyond
civilization—
give her a seat
in the camphor tree
by your study,

for she can give tongue
to the reveries of trees
and what
that mountain
commands…[30]

---

30  Lowinsky, First published in *Weber Studies*.

Well, it's certainly true that Rima has been my muse out here in the suburbs; poetry keeps coming and I live in the presence of a sacred mountain. But what can poetry do when catastrophe looms?

Earth Angel responds: *Poetry amplifies the Great Song of creation—the song begun by Grandmother Spider and the Sun. Poetry sings of the spirit of place—the love humans have for their Earth Angel, their homeland. It expresses the love you have for all the places you travel, like the little fishing village in Mexico you and Dan visit every winter to reweave your soul into the sounds of the sea, the sight of the pelicans dipping their wings in the waves and whales leaping and spouting off in the distance. Or Venice, which you recently visited, and where you learned much about human resilience and survival in a borderland area that belongs to the sea. Ironically, it was Venice that gave you the state of grace created by an environment without cars. You felt released from the relentless physical pressure and curtain of noise that you didn't even know plagued you; you felt returned to your walking self, to "a sensuous world that had been waiting, for years, at the very fringe of our awareness, an intimate terrain infused by birdsong, salt spray, and the light of stars" to borrow from David Abram.*[31]

*Abram understands, as poets do, that poetry reaches down to the carnal nature of language, to the physical ground of our being, through the way "words feel in the mouth or roll off the tongue…—the taste of a word or a phrase, the way it modulates the body…"*[32] *Poetry, says Abram, weaves together poet and listener/reader in a sensuous web of mutual experience. Poets are the makers of "wild, living…language."*

> Actual, living speech is…a vocal gesticulation wherein the meaning is inseparable from the sound, the shape, and the rhythm of the words…It remains rooted in the sensual dimension of experience born of the body's native capacity to resonate with other bodies and with the landscape as a whole.[33]

*What Abram understands,* Earth Angel continues, *is that poetry is as much a manifestation of me, your Earth Angel, your Earth Spirit, your*

---

31  Abram, *Spell of the Sensuous*, p. 61.
32  Abram, *Spell of the Sensuous*, p. 81.
33  Abram, *Spell of the Sensuous*, p. 72.

*Grandmother Spider, as is your poem. We all depend on the great web of language—how words connect back to older words, to ancient languages—Sanskrit, Greek, Latin, Old English, Middle German—bringing ancient wisdom to consciousness. If you trace the roots of the word Spider you find Old English, Germanic, Latin and Greek roots that weave dissimilar words together: spin, depend, suspend, weigh, toil. The spider is suspended from Her thread. We all depend on Her toil. As Grandmother Spider extrudes Her thread out of Her body so do the lines of a poem emerge out of the poet's body—her breath, her vision, her inner ear. The poem is a living thing. The poet has to weigh each word, each beat; she has to suspend her will so the poem can find its own way, own shape, own resonance. It demands much of its maker, wrestling with her in the night like a singing demon, catching her in the web of language and devouring her until it finds its right rhythm, right form, right imagery.*

*I'm telling you, the right poem can wake up the poet and all those the poem touches to remember our place in the natural world and our love for the Earth and all its creatures. Maybe that's why so many people are writing poetry these days. You hunger for a poetry that returns you to your senses, to your animal nature, your vegetable and mineral nature.*

## An Amulet of Feather and Fin

> *If we could create an amulet…*
> *of feather and fin, of marsh grass and mystical measures*
> *of dolphin song, could we bring back the deep sea roe*

*Remember the terrible BP oil spill in the Gulf of Mexico in 2010? It was one of the worst oil disasters in history. Over 8,000 animals were reported dead in the first six months and it is still polluting the coastline. You were overcome with grief and reached out to the web of poets you read to invoke Pattiann Rogers, a naturalist and a fine poet:*

## Invoking Pattiann Rogers During the Oil Spill

If I knew as much science as you, Pattiann

the migratory patterns, mating rituals, feeding behavior
of all those creatures engulfed in sludge
would be in this poem.  Would that help
those whose feathers are encrusted in crude
those whose webbed feet can't swim
those with gaping mouths—dead on the beach?

If I had your Audubon eye—to describe how the least tern
sits on her eggs, how the pelican makes her nest—
could we protect their hatchlings?  Could we rescue

the oil clogged sea turtle, the laughing gull
the meandering crab dodging balls of tar, with poems?

Me?  I get visions, and their unbearable
music—there's a dragonfly with oil
weighted wings, there's a blackened egret…
This is a dirge for the bluefin tuna—
They've lost their spawning grounds
in an ocean gone mad with black blood

If we could create an amulet, Pattiann
of feather and fin, of marsh grass and mystical measures
of dolphin song, could we bring back the deep sea roe
or are we washed up too
in the Gulf
between how we are all connected—pelicans, poets, bluefin tuna—
                                  and what has become of our world?[34]

It's been four years since the BP Oil spill in the Gulf of Mexico. It's been twenty-five years since the Exon Valdez spill in Alaska. The herring and the fishermen have never recovered. Just last year an oil tanker collision in Galveston Bay released 168,000 gallons of fuel oil into the Gulf of Mexico. It keeps on happening. I feel flooded, polluted, exhausted. What can poetry do?

*You have a book in your library called "Can Poetry Save the Earth?" "First consciousness, then conscience," writes the book's editor John Felstin-*

---

[34] Lowinsky, first published in *The Book of Now,* ed. Leah Shelleda.

er.[35] I know it's depressing and overwhelming. But you know things don't happen in a linear causal way. Changes come out of left field, a song in your head, a dream, something you stumble on in the woods when you're walking with Dan. Remember? His curiosity, his always wanting to go off the beaten path, led you to that labyrinth that surprised you—an unexpected gift from an unseen ally.

I love that labyrinth, I entered with my question: "How do I approach helping Earth?" The pathways in this labyrinth are narrow, with hairpin curves that throw me off balance. I heard the voice of the Earth: "Balance. That's what it is all about. Your balance, my balance. It's a constantly shifting practice, staying in balance."

A dad and his son approached. "Oh no," I thought, "noise and disruption." To my surprise the father spoke to his son: "This is the same kind of labyrinth they have at Grace Cathedral. You can walk it. But if you enter you have to stick to it, until you get to the center, or it's bad luck." The youngster, who was just at the edge of puberty, entered the labyrinth in a focused and respectful way. His lithe young body had no difficulty with the curves and the tricks—the places where you thought you were almost there and were suddenly flung out to the edge. He was much faster than I. I was happy to let him pass, moved that he was being initiated into this ancient mystery practice, glad his dad said, "you have to make an offering, even if it's just a hair from your head." The boy waited for me to get to the center and watched. I picked up a small stone and put it on a rock. He did the same. Then he leapt out with a shy smile at me. But I, being a pilgrim, had to wend my way back out through all the arches and curves, listening to Earth speak to my inner ear of how the labyrinth—though it teases and confuses—will lead you. "It is a sacred form, a human web that weaves you back into a wisdom your ancestors painted on cave walls." I heard Earth singing: "Earth Angel, will you be mine?" Suddenly, Dan called my name. He was pointing to a white presence moving swiftly across the meadow, into the woods. "Coyote!"

Back home in my study I found my *Encyclopedia of Archetypal Symbolism* and read these words of my late mentor, Joseph Henderson—a

---

35  John Felstiner, *Can Poetry Save the Earth?* p. xiii.

founding member of the San Francisco Institute—which describe my experience in the labyrinth, and perhaps, the nature of our journey back to Earth. "The experience of the labyrinth…temporarily disturbs rational conscious orientation…the initiate is 'confused' and symbolically 'loses his way.' Yet, in this descent to chaos, the inner mind is opened to the awareness of a new cosmic dimension of a transcendent nature."[36]

The world is still as big a mess as it was before I entered that labyrinth. But I feel more balanced, rewoven into earth and soul. As Jung says:

> People who have got dirty through too much civilization take a walk in the woods, or a bath in the sea…They…allow nature to touch them. It can be done within or without. Walking in the woods, lying on the grass, taking a bath in the sea, are from the outside; entering the unconscious, entering yourself through dreams, is touching nature from the inside and this is the same thing, things are put right again.[37]

---

36 Joseph Henderson in *An Encyclopedia of Archetypal Symbolism*, ed. Beverly Moon p. 68.
37 Jung, *The Earth has a Soul*, ed. Meredith Sabini, pp. 207-8.

# BIBLIOGRAPHY

*A Flowering Tree.* Libretto by John Adams and Peter Sellars, Music by John Adams. Not published. 2006

Abram, David. *The Spell of the Sensuous: Perception and Language in a More-Than-Human World.* New York: Vintage eBooks, 1997.

Allen, Paula Gunn. *The Sacred Hoop: Recovering the Feminine in American Indian Traditions.* Boston: Beacon Press, 1986.

Auger, Janine, JAP, Vol. 31, 1986.

Bly, Robert. *Leaping Poetry: An Idea With Poems and Translations.* Pittsburgh: University of Pittsburgh Press, 1975.

Brooks, Christopher A. & Sims, Robert. *Roland Hayes: The Legacy of an American Tenor.* Bloomington: Indiana University Press, 2015.

Chaplin, Patrice. *City of Secrets: One Woman's True-life Journey to the Heart of the Grail Legend.* Wheaton, Illinois: Quest Books, 2008.

Chief Seattle, http://thinkexist.com/quotes/chief_seattle/

Coetzee, J.M., *Disgrace.* New York: Penguin Books, 1999.

Cooper, David A. *God is a Verb.* New York: Riverhead Books, 1997.

Daniélou, Alain. *The Myths and Gods of India.* Rochester, Vermont: Inner Traditions International, 1991.

Duberman, Martin. *Black Mountain: An Exploration in Community.* New York: W.W. Norton, 1993.

Edelstein, Jillian. (Ed.) *Truth and Lies: Stories from the Truth and Reconciliation Commission in South Africa.* New York: The New Press, 2001.

Edinger, Edward. *Goethe's Faust: Notes for a Jungian Commentary.* Toronto: Inner City Books, 1990.

Fortune, Dion. *The Mystical Qabalah.* York Beach, Maine, 2000.

Funk, Wilfred. *Word Origins.* New York: Bell Publishing, 1978.

Gerber, Jane S. *The Jews of Spain: A History of the Sephardic Experience.* New York: The Free Press, 1992.

Gimbutas, Marija. *The Language of the Goddess.* San Francisco: Harper & Row, 1989.

Graves, Robert. *The White Goddess.* New York: Farrar, Straus and Giroux, 1975.

Hall, Donald. (Ed.) "What the Image Can Do," *Claims for Poetry.* Ann Arbor: The University of Michigan Press, 1995.

Harris, Mary Emma. *The Arts at Black Mountain.* Cambridge: MIT Press, 1987.

Hayden, Robert. *Collected Poems.* New York: Liveright Publishing, 1985.

Hayden, Robert C. *Singing for All People.* Boston: Select Publications, 1989.

Hayes, Roland. *My Favorite Spirituals.* Mineola, NY: Dover, 2001.

Heaney, Seamus. *Opened Ground.* New York: Farrar, Straus and Giroux, 1998.

Helm, Mackinley. *Angel Mo' and Her Son Roland Hayes.* Boston: Little, Brown and Company, 1945.

Hildegard of Bingen, *Meditations with Hildegard of Bingen.* Rochester, Vermont: Bear & Co., 1983.

Hirsch, Edward. *How to Read a Poem and Fall in Love with Poetry.* New York: Harcourt, Brace and Company, 1999.

Hirshfield, Jane. (Ed.) *Women in Praise of the Sacred.* New York: HarperCollins, 1994.

Hirson, Denis. (Ed.) *The Lava of this Land: South African Poetry 1960-1996.* Evanston, Illinois: Northwestern University Press, 1997.

Hoagland, Tony. *Real Sofistikashun: Essays on Poetry and Craft.* Saint Paul: Gray Wolf, 2006.

IAAP Conference Proceedings: Capetown 2007.

Idel, Moshe & Ostrow, Mortimer. *Jewish Mystical Leaders and Leadership in the 13th Century.* Lanham, Maryland: Jason Aronson, Inc., 1994.

Johnson, Buffie. *Lady of the Beasts.* San Francisco: Harper & Row, 1988.

Jung, C.G. *The Collected Works,* Vols. 5-6, 9i-9ii, 11-15, 17. (R.F.C. Hull, (Trans.) Princeton: Princeton University Press, 1978.

_____ *Letters,* Vol. I. Princeton: Princeton University Press, 1973.

_____ *Letters,* Vol. II. Princeton: Princeton University Press, 1991.

_____ *Memories, Dreams, Reflections.* New York: Vintage Books, 1965.

_____ *Man and His Symbols.* New York: Doubleday, 1964.

_____ *The Red Book.* New York W.W. Norton and Company, 2009.

Jung, C.G. & C. Kerenyi. *Essays on a Science of Mythology*. Princeton: Bollingen Series XII, Princeton University Press, 1959.

Karcher, Stephen. "Re-enchanting the Mind," *Psychological Perspectives*, Vol. 50, #2.

Kimbles, Samuel. *Phantom Narratives: The Unseen Contributions of Culture to Psyche*. London: Rowman & Littlefield, 2014.

Krog, Antjie. *Body Bereft*, Houghton, South Africa: Umuzi, 2006

Kundera, Milan. *Immortality*. New York: HarperCollins, 1990.

Lorde, Audre. *The Collected Poems of Audre Lorde*. New York: W.W. Norton, 1997.

Lowinsky, Naomi Ruth. *adagio & lamentation: poems*. Carmel, CA: Fisher King Press, 2010.

_____ *crimes of the dreamer: poems*. Oakland: Scarlet Tanager Books, 2005.

_____ *The Faust Woman Poems*. Carmel, CA: Fisher King Press, 2013.

_____ *The Little House on Stilts Remembers: Poems*. San Francisco: Blue Light Press, 2015.

_____ *The Motherline: Every Woman's Journey to Find Her Female Roots*. Carmel, CA: Fisher King Press, 2009.

_____ *red clay is talking: poems* Oakland, CA: Scarlet Tanager Books, 2000.

_____ *The Sister from Below: When the Muse Gets Her Way*. Carmel, CA: Fisher King Press, 2009.

Lowinsky, Naomi Ruth & Damery, Patricia. *Marked by Fire: Stories of the Jungian Way*. Carmel, CA: Fisher King Press, 2012.

Matt, Daniel C. T*he Essential Kabbalah: The Heart of Jewish Mysticism*. HarperSanFrancisco, 1996.

Matthews, Caitlin. *Sophia: Goddess of Wisdom, Bride of God*. Wheaton, Illinois: Quest Books, 2001.

McGuire, William & R.F.C. Hull. (Eds.) *C.G. Jung Speaking: Interviews and Encounters*. Princeton: Princeton University Press, 1977.

Metzger, Deena. *Writing for Your Life*. HarperSanFrancisco, 1992.

Moon, Beverly. (Ed.) *An Encyclopedia of Archetypal Symbolism*. Boston: Shambhala, 1991.

Mozart's *Magic Flute*. (n.d.), Quoted in Grand Lodge of British Columbia and Yukon, http://www.freemasonry.bcy.ca/biography/_a/mozarts_magic_flute.html.

Nicholson, Shirley. *The Goddess Re-Awakening: The Feminine Principle Today*. Wheaton, Illinois: The Theosophical Publishing House.

Raff, Jeffrey. *Jung and the Alchemical Imagination*. York Beach, ME: Nicolas-Hays, 2000.

_____ *The Wedding of Sophia: The Divine Feminine in Psychoidal Alchemy*. Berwick, ME: Nicolas-Hays, 2003.

Ramanujan, A.K. *A Flowering Tree and Other Tales*. University of California Press, 1997.

_____ *Collected Essays*. Oxford: Oxford University Press, 1999.

_____ *Collected Poems*. Oxford: Oxford University Press, 1995.

_____ *When God Is a Customer*. Berkeley: University of California Press, 1996.

Raphael, Alice. *Goethe and the Philosopher's Stone*. New York: Garret Publications, 1965.

Roszak, Theodore. *The Voice of the Earth: An Exploration of Ecopsychology*. Grand Rapids, MI.: Phanes Press, 2001.

Salopek, Paul. "A Stroll Around the World," *New York Times Sunday Review*, November 24, 2013.

Scholem, Gershom. *Major Trends in Jewish Mysticism*. New York: Schocken Books, 1995.

_____ *On the Kabbalah and Its Symbolism*. New York: Schocken Books, 1996.

Schwartz, Howard. *Tree of Souls: The Mythology of Judaism*. Oxford: Oxford University Press, 2004.

Serote, Mongane Wally. *Freedom, Lament and Song*, Cape Town: David Philip Publishers, 1997.

Shelleda, Leah. (Ed.) T*he Book of Now: Poetry for the Rising Tide*. Carmel, CA: Fisher King Press, 2012.

Shlain, Leonard. *The Alphabet Versus the Goddess: The Conflict Between Word and Image*. New York: Viking, 1998.

Somé, Malidoma. *Of Water and the Spirit*. New York: Penguin Compass, 1994.

Southern, Eileen, *The Music of Black Americans.* New York: W.W. Norton & Co. 1997.

Tagore, Rabindranath. *Gitanjali.* Delhi, India: International Pocket Library. 1992.

*The Bible*, King James Version. New York: Abradale Press, 1965.

*The Common English Bible.* Nashville, Tennessee: Church Resources Development Corporation, 2011.

*The Magic Flute.* Libretto by Emanuel Schikaneder. Music composed by W.A. Mozart.

Tutu, Desmond. *No Future without Forgiveness.* New York: Doubleday, 2000.

von Franz, Marie-Louise. *Alchemy.* Toronto: Inner City Books, 1981.

von Goethe, Johann Wolfgang. *Faust: A Norton Critical Edition.* Translated by Walter Arndt. New York: W.W. Norton, 1976.

_____ *Faust.* Translated by Barker Fairley. Toronto: University of Toronto Press, 1985.

_____ *Faust.* Translated by Walter Kaufmann. New York: Anchor Books, 1961.

_____ *Faust.* Translated by David Luke, Parts I & II. Oxford: Oxford University Press, 2008.

_____ *Selected Verse.* (Ed. David Luke) London: Penguin, 1964.

Wright, Charles. *A Short History of the Shadow: Poems.* New York: Farrar, Straus, Giroux, 2002.

Young, Al. *Heaven: Collected Poems 1956-1990.* Berkeley: Creative Arts Book Company, 1992.

Zimmer, Heinrich. *Myths and Symbols in Indian Art and Civilization.* Princeton: Mythos, 1992.

Ziolkowski, Theodore. *The Sin of Knowledge: Ancient Themes and Modern Variations.* Princeton: Princeton University Press, 2000.

CDs:

The Art of Roland Hayes. Smithsonian Collection of Recordings.

Charlton Heston reads from The Life and Passion of Jesus Christ. Roland Hayes: Aframerican Religious Songs. Vanguard Classics

# INDEX

## A

Abram, David 198, 199, 200, 210
Acharontos 74, 75
active imagination 21, 61, 62, 63, 110, 111, 118, 163, 180, 181
Adams, John
  *A Flowering Tree* 26, 27, 28, 29, 32, 33, 35, 36, 37, 38, 39, 42, 43, 215, 218
albedo 75
Alchemical Imagination 66, 218
alchemical opus 85
alchemical writings 40
alchemist(s) 2, 47, 51, 52, 57, 59, 60, 62, 65, 73, 75, 84, 93
alchemy 1, 48, 60, 61, 62, 65, 71, 73, 74, 79, 80, 81, 111, 164
American life 11
Anderson, Marian 105, 157
angel (fallen) 200
angels 74, 93, 98, 111, 124
*anima* 26, 29, 79, 89, 92, 98, 178, 179, 197
anti-apartheid 143
Antichrist 95
apartheid 131, 134, 135, 137, 138, 142, 143, 144, 145, 149
Asawa, Ruth 104
Asherah 39
Atom bomb 97
*axis mundi* 9

## B

Bach 103, 105, 116, 117, 123, 127, 128, 202
beggar 36
beggars 37
Bentley, Eric 107, 108
Bhagavad Gita 40
Biko, Stephen 131, 133
Black Mountain College 104, 105, 106, 107, 108, 109, 117, 120, 121, 129, 150, 201, 202, 215, 216
Bly, Robert 14, 15, 18, 215
Bollingen 42, 217
Book of Life 196
BP oil spill 211
Buber, Martin 1
Buddha 24, 34, 40

## C

Cage, John 104
call of the wild 65
Cally Berry 193
Cape Town 132, 133, 135, 137, 138, 139, 140, 141, 142, 150, 218
Celtic wisdom 21
Chaos 194, 202
Chopin 127
Christian worldview 88
circumambulation 27
Codex Marianus 74
collaboration of the unconscious 11
cornucopia of life 98
Cossacks 131
creative imagination 26, 34
creative process 21, 90
creative spirit 2
Creeley, Robert 104, 106
cultural stories 103

Cunningham, Merce 104

## D

dark goddess 10, 27, 30, 34
dark night of the soul 1
de Leon, Moses 168
demons 20, 161
Devil's Peak 132, 139
divine energy 41
divine images 94
Duberman, Martin 107, 108, 109, 215
Duncan, Robert 104, 106

## E

Earth Day 43
earthquake 11, 51
ecstasy 51, 52, 103, 173, 181, 188
Edinger, Edward 42, 47, 48, 61, 66, 78, 87, 88, 89, 94, 95, 96, 215
*enantiodromia* 95
esse in anima 26, 29
Euphorion 92

## F

fallopian tubes 10
fantasies 12, 21, 22, 178, 179
fascism 127
Faust 25, 42, 78, 79, 80, 82, 83, 84, 85, 86, 87, 88, 89, 90, 91, 92, 93, 94, 95, 96, 97, 98, 99, 100, 160, 196, 197, 215, 217, 219
fire 6, 10, 16, 17, 20, 44, 47, 48, 93, 98, 125, 148, 162, 169, 170, 173, 174, 176, 177, 178, 179, 180, 181, 183, 184, 186, 187, 188, 189, 190, 206, 207, 208, 209
Fisk University 113

Flowering Tree 26, 27, 28, 29, 32, 33, 34, 35, 36, 37, 38, 39, 42, 43, 215, 218
folklore 9, 29, 106
Frantz, Gilda 180
Freud 91, 177
funda 48, 64, 73, 75, 178

## G

Gandhi 129
Ganesha 11
Garden of Eden 41, 87
Gilgamesh 14, 80
Gimbutas, Marija 10, 215
Gnosticism 62
Gobodo-Madikizela, Pumla 136, 137, 138, 143, 144, 145
god of the forest 34
Goethe 28, 42, 78, 79, 80, 81, 82, 83, 84, 86, 87, 88, 89, 90, 91, 92, 93, 94, 95, 96, 98, 100, 179, 196, 197, 215, 218, 219
Gould, Baruch 43
Grace Cathedral 213
Graves, Robert 6, 7, 8, 22
Great Goddess 124
Great Recession 89
guilt 41, 42, 98, 136, 146, 206

## H

Hamlet 78
Hayes, Roland 103, 104, 105, 106, 109, 111, 112, 113, 114, 115, 116, 117, 118, 119, 121, 122, 124, 129, 150, 157, 216, 219, 220
Helen of Troy 96
Henderson, Joseph 48, 64, 86, 177, 178, 194, 213, 214
hermetic philosophy 106

Hildegard of Bingen  8, 216
Hinduism  7, 165
Hirsch, Edward  23, 216
Holy Spirit  6, 20
Homunculus  85, 88, 92
Horus  74, 111

## I

Icarus  92
Inanna  18
Indra  193
inner life  12, 14, 111, 163, 176, 206, 207
irreverent  20
Isis  74, 75, 111, 120, 121, 124

## J

Jewish mysticism  8, 63, 163
Joyce, James
  *Portrait of the Artist as a Young Man*  62
Judaism  22, 39, 110, 155, 165, 166, 218
Jung, C.G.
  *Answer to Job*  145, 166
  *Man and His Symbols*  50, 86, 177, 198, 200, 216
  *Memories, Dreams, Reflections*  78, 79, 165, 178, 216
  *Mysterium Coniunctionis*  47, 94, 164, 166, 174
  *The Red Book*  1, 176, 177, 178, 179, 180, 181, 182, 184, 188, 189, 216
Jung, Emma  22, 178
Jung's mother  79

## K

Kabbalah  , 22, 41, 62, 63, 71, 150, 155, 157, 163, 164, 165, 167, 169, 170, ix, 218
Kabbalistic  9, 150, 164, 167
Kabbalists  42, 167
Kabir  38
Kali  11, 30
Karo, Rabbi Joseph  166
Kimbles, Samuel  126, 146, 217
King, Martin Luther  129, 133, 159
Koran  40
Krishna  11
Ku Klux Klan  105
Kumudha  31, 32, 33, 34, 35, 36, 37, 38, 42, 43

## L

labyrinth  213, 214
Lady of Healing  111
Lady Tree  2, 5, 7, 8, 10, 11, 15, 18, 19, 20, 21, 22, 23, 25, 207
Lawrence, Jacob  104
Lesbos  18
libido  10, 19, 20, 79, 91, 94, 181
living psyche  1
living symbol  6, 8, 9, 10, 11, 17, 18, 19, 20, 23
longissima via  56
Lowinsky, Noami Ruth
  *Sister from Below*  2, 8, 15, 21, 22, 161, 162, 170, 174, 180, 181, 188, 189, 217

## M

Malcolm X  133
Mandela, Nelson  131, 134, 135, 140, 146, 147
*massa confusa*  51, 52, 61
Maya  39, 40
Meador, Betty  68
Mephistopheles  80, 84, 85, 86, 87, 88, 89, 90, 91, 92, 93, 95, 196

Merwin, W.S. 76, 207
Messer, Richard 194
Metzger, Deena 9, 12, 20, 23, 217
Middle Ages 8, 18, 40
Moravian Brethren 81
Mother Earth 34, 43, 204
Mozart 27, 28, 103, 116, 120, 121, 123, 127, 218, 219
  *The Magic Flute* 27, 28, 42, 43, 44, 219
musicologist 7, 104, 180
mysticism 8, 63, 163, 169
mythology 106

# N

Nahman, Rabbi Moses ben (Ramban) 168, 169, 170, 171, 172, 173, 174
Naskapi Indians 50, 53, 61, 74
Nazis 131, 138, 143, 146, 158, 197
Neptune 194
nigredo 1, 51, 67
Nobel Peace Prize 43
numinosum 94

# O

Olson, Charles 104, 106
Origen 66

# P

Pan 21
Panpipe 28
Paracelsus 61, 66, 81, 96
Paris and Helen 85, 89, 91, 92, 94
Parvati 31
Passover 106
patriarchal worldview 9
Perun 193
Philosophical Tree 18, 21, 22, 39, 40, 41, 164

Poseidon 193
*prima materia* 66, 67, 111
primordial roots 9
Prometheus 88, 96

# Q

Queen of Sheba 62
Queen of the Night 26, 27, 31, 32, 40, 42

# R

Raff, Jeffrey 66, 166, 218
Ramanujan, A.K. 26, 27, 29, 30, 32, 34, 37, 38, 39, 41, 218
Renaissance 7, 96, 158, 180
reproductive organs 10
reproductive years 48
Robeson, Paul 105, 157
*Rosarium* 60, 81
*Rosarium philosophorum* 81

# S

sanctuary 19, 20
San Francisco Jung Institute 1, 47, 130
Sappho 18, 76, 148
Sarasvati 7, 11
Scholem, Gershom 167, 169, 170, 171, 218
*Secret of the Golden Flower* 21
Shakti 31
Shalit, Erel 138
shamanic initiation 22
shameful 20, 195
Shango 193
shape-shifting 8, 35, 201
Shekinah 41, 165, 166, 167, 170
Shiva 31, 181
Shlain, Leonard 162, 218
Shoah 126, 145, 146, 183, 188

Somé, Malidoma  8, 22
soothsayer  55
Sophia  61, 62, 63, 65, 66, 69, 71, 74, 110, 111, 116, 117, 118, 120, 122, 124, 166, 217, 218
sorcerer  95, 138
South Africa  125, 126, 129, 131, 132, 133, 143, 145, 215, 217
Sufi dances  73
Susanowo  193

## T

Table Mountain  132, 135, 139
taboo  19, 20, 200
Tagore, Rabindranath  42, 219
Tarot  20
temples at Jaipur  18
terminating an analysis  2, 110
Thor  193
"Tikkun Olam"  42
Tohu Bohu  193, 194, 196
transcendent function  53
transformation  33, 34, 36, 39, 41, 50, 51, 52, 75, 91, 95, 126, 145, 174
Tree Alphabet  8, 21
Tree of Life  8, 9, 22, 41, 163, 166, 178
Troubadour songs  73
Tutu, Desmond  131, 132, 138, 219
Twelve Apostles  132

## U

underworld  9, 14, 43, 68, 75, 79, 92
uterus  10

## V

von Franz, Marie-Louise  50, 61, 62, 66, 67, 74, 106, 111, 116, 219

## W

wandering soul  14
Wangari Muta  43
war-mongering  42
White Goddess  6, 7, 8, 22, 216
widening of consciousness  51, 53

## Y

Yom Kippur  163

## Z

Zimmer, Heinrich  26, 125, 219

# You might also enjoy reading:

*Marked By Fire: Stories of the Jungian Way* edited by Patricia Damery & Naomi Ruth Lowinsky, 1st Ed., Trade Paperback, 180pp, Biblio., 2012
— ISBN 978-1-926715-68-1

*The Dream and Its Amplification* edited by Erel Shalit & Nancy Swift Furlotti, 1st Ed., Trade Paperback, 180pp, Biblio., 2013
— ISBN 978-1-926715-89-6

*Shared Realities: Participation Mystique and Beyond* edited by Mark Winborn, 1st Ed., Trade Paperback, 270pp, Index, Biblio., 2014
— ISBN 978-1-77169-009-6

*Pierre Teilhard de Chardin and C.G. Jung: Side by Side* edited by Fred Gustafson, 1st Ed., Trade Paperback, 270pp, Index, Biblio., 2014
— ISBN 978-1-77169-014-0

*Re-Imagining Mary: A Journey Through Art to the Feminine Self* by Mariann Burke, 1st Ed., Trade Paperback, 180pp, Index, Biblio., 2009
— ISBN 978-0-9810344-1-6

*Advent and Psychic Birth* by Mariann Burke, Revised Ed., Trade Paperback, 170pp, 2014
— ISBN 978-1-926715-99-5

*Transforming Body and Soul* by Steven Galipeau, Rev. Ed., Trade Paperback, 180pp, Index, Biblio., 2011
— ISBN 978-1-926715-62-9

*Lifting the Veil: Revealing the Other Side* by Fred Gustafson & Jane Kamerling, 1st Ed., Trade Paperback, 170pp, Biblio., 2012
— ISBN 978-1-926715-75-9

*Resurrecting the Unicorn: Masculinity in the 21st Century* by Bud Harris, Rev. Ed., Trade Paperback, 300pp, Index, Biblio., 2009
— ISBN 978-0-9810344-0-9

*The Father Quest: Rediscovering an Elemental Force* by Bud Harris, Reprint, Trade Paperback, 180pp, Index, Biblio., 2009
— ISBN 978-0-9810344-9-2

*Like Gold Through Fire: The Transforming Power of Suffering* by Massimilla & Bud Harris, Reprint, Trade Paperback, 150pp, Index, Biblio., 2009 — ISBN 978-0-9810344-5-4

*The Art of Love: The Craft of Relationship* by Massimilla and Bud Harris, 1st Ed., Trade Paperback, 150pp, 2010
— ISBN 978-1-926715-02-5

*Divine Madness: Archetypes of Romantic Love* by John R. Haule, Rev. Ed., Trade Paperback, 282pp, Index, Biblio., 2010
— ISBN 978-1-926715-04-9

*Tantra and Erotic Trance in 2 volumes* by John R. Haule
  *Volume 1 - Outer Work,* 1st Ed., Trade Paperback, 215pp, Index, Bibliography, 2012 — ISBN 978-0-9776076-8-6
  *Volume 2 - Inner Work,* 1st Ed., Trade Paperback, 215pp, Index, Bibliography, 2012 — ISBN 978-0-9776076-9-3

*Eros and the Shattering Gaze: Transcending Narcissism*
by Ken Kimmel, 1st Ed., Trade Paperback, 310pp, Index, Biblio., 2011 — ISBN 978-1-926715-49-0

*The Sister From Below: When the Muse Gets Her Way*
by Naomi Ruth Lowinsky, 1st Ed., Trade Paperback, 248pp, Index, Biblio., 2009 — ISBN 978-0-9810344-2-3

*The Motherline: Every Woman's Journey to Find Her Female Roots*
by Naomi Ruth Lowinsky, Reprint, Trade Paperback, 252pp, Index, Biblio., 2009 — ISBN 978-0-9810344-6-1

*The Dairy Farmer's Guide to the Universe in 4 volumes*
by Dennis L. Merritt:
  *Volume 1 - Jung and Ecopsychology,* 1st Ed., Trade Paperback, 242pp, Index, Biblio., 2011 — ISBN 978-1-926715-42-1
  *Volume 2 - The Cry of Merlin: Jung the Prototypical Ecopsychologist,* 1st Ed., Trade Paperback, 204pp, Index, Biblio., 2012 — ISBN 978-1-926715-43-8
  *Volume 3 - Hermes, Ecopsychology, and Complexity Theory,* 1st Ed., Trade Paperback, 228pp, Index, Biblio., 2012 — ISBN 978-1-926715-44-5
  *Volume 4 - Land, Weather, Seasons, Insects: An Archetypal View,* 1st Ed., Trade Paperback, 134pp, Index, Biblio., 2012 — ISBN 978-1-926715-45-2

*Four Eternal Women: Toni Wolff Revisited—A Study In Opposites*
by Mary Dian Molton & Lucy Anne Sikes, 1st Ed., 320pp, Index, Biblio., 2011 — ISBN 978-1-926715-31-5

*Becoming: An Introduction to Jung's Concept of Individuation*
by Deldon Anne McNeely, 1st Ed., Trade Paperback, 230pp, Index, Biblio., 2010 — ISBN 978-1-926715-12-4

*Animus Aeternus: Exploring the Inner Masculine* by Deldon Anne McNeely, Reprint, Trade Paperback, 196pp, Index, Biblio., 2011 — ISBN 978-1-926715-37-7

*Mercury Rising: Women, Evil, and the Trickster Gods*
by Deldon Anne McNeely, Revised, Trade Paperback, 200pp, Index, Biblio., 2011 — ISBN 978-1-926715-54-4

*Gathering the Light: A Jungian View of Meditation*
by V. Walter Odajnyk, Revised Ed., Trade Paperback, 264pp, Index, Biblio., 2011 — ISBN 978-1-926715-55-1

*The Promiscuity Papers*
by Matjaz Regovec, 1st Ed., Trade Paperback, 86pp, Index, Biblio., 2011 — ISBN 978-1-926715-38-4

*Enemy, Cripple, Beggar: Shadows in the Hero's Path*
by Erel Shalit, 1st Ed., Trade Paperback, 248pp, Index, Biblio., 2008 — ISBN 978-0-9776076-7-9

*The Cycle of Life: Themes and Tales of the Journey*
by Erel Shalit, 1st Ed., Trade Paperback, 210pp, Index, Biblio., 2011 — ISBN 978-1-926715-50-6

*The Hero and His Shadow*
by Erel Shalit, Revised Ed., Trade Paperback, 208pp, Index, Biblio., 2012 — ISBN 978-1-926715-69-8

*Riting Myth, Mythic Writing: Plotting Your Personal Story*
by Dennis Patrick Slattery, Trade Paperback, 220 pp. Biblio., 2012 — ISBN 978-1-926715-77-3

*The Guilt Cure*
by Nancy Carter Pennington & Lawrence H. Staples, 1st Ed., Trade Paperback, 200pp, Index, Biblio., 2011 — ISBN 978-1-926715-53-7

*Guilt with a Twist: The Promethean Way*
by Lawrence Staples, 1st Ed., Trade Paperback, 256pp, Index, Biblio., 2008 — ISBN 978-0-9776076-4-8

*The Creative Soul: Art and the Quest for Wholeness*
by Lawrence Staples, 1st Ed., Trade Paperback, 100pp, Index, Biblio., 2009 — ISBN 978-0-9810344-4-7

*Deep Blues: Human Soundscapes for the Archetypal Journey*
by Mark Winborn, 1st Ed., Trade Paperback, 130pp, Index, Biblio., 2011 — ISBN 978-1-926715-52-0

Phone Orders Welcomed
Credit Cards Accepted
In Canada & the U.S. call 1-800-228-9316
International call +1-831-238-7799
www.fisherkingpress.com

www.ingramcontent.com/pod-product-compliance
Lightning Source LLC
Chambersburg PA
CBHW022010220426
43663CB00007B/1025